THE
PEOPLE'S
BREWER

Anna-Lise Bjerager

THE PEOPLE'S BREWER

Gyldendal

THE PEOPLE'S BREWER
By Anna-Lise Bjerager

By the same author
Bryggerens lærling, Povl Krogsgaard-Larsens erindringer (2011)

© 2011 Anna-Lise Bjerager and Gyldendal A/S
Image editing: Bodil Hammer
English translation/editing & proofreading:
Borella projects
Cover and typesetting: Søren Damstedt,
Trefold
Printing: Narayana Press

ISBN: 978-87-00-78859-6
Special edition

This book has been produced with the
support of the Carlsberg Foundation.

Printed in Denmark

Gyldendal Business
Klareboderne 3
1001 Copenhagen K
Denmark
Tel.: +45 33 75 55 55
www.GyldendalBusiness.dk

CONTENTS

FOREWORD

Can we really learn anything from the past? And if we can, is it not mostly the acknowledged great thinkers who have something to teach us? In Denmark, Søren Kierkegaard, for example, the great philosopher who taught us that life can only be understood backwards but must be lived forwards. Or the writer Hans Christian Andersen, who told us that life is a fairy tale.

J.C. Jacobsen, the brewer who was a contemporary of both Søren Kierkegaard and Hans Christian Andersen, would no doubt have been astonished to know that two hundred years after his birth he would be mentioned in the same breath as philosophers and writers. He did not consider himself of the same calibre. Yet it is the assertion of this book that we can still learn much today from a humble brewer, for the fact is that in all his practical doings J.C. Jacobsen was an example to be followed.

The industrialisation and major political upheavals of which J.C. Jacobsen and his contemporaries were a part in the nineteenth century helped pave the way for the Danish society which we know and love today. But something seems to have been lost along the way, so it is worth taking the trouble to look a little closer at what it actually was that J.C. Jacobsen did all those years ago. His altruistic business ethic, embodied in the resolve that the money he made from beer should benefit society and the common good, certainly deserves reconsideration.

We live in a time when individualism, one of the essentially positive "isms" which arose in J.C. Jacobsen's century and which has brought about so much good through its emphasis on the special attributes and worth of the individual, is in danger of getting out of hand. The modern individual risks becoming his or her own project, disconnected from the contexts of family, friends, workplace and community at a cost of increased loneliness and dissatisfaction. In the business world, the ugly side of this tendency has manifested itself all too predictably during the recent financial crisis: throughout the western world there have been depressing examples of unlawful personal enrichment and other unethical conduct at corporate management level.

For J.C. Jacobsen, however, money was never a goal in itself. It was a means to improve the functioning of his brewery while at the same time supporting a number of socially beneficial causes through the Carlsberg Foundation. People who were in financial need could count on J.C. Jacobsen, whether it was a family which had lost a father to war or an actor who needed to convalesce abroad. And he was also able to deliver practical help, such as offering advice to other brewers, building a school, or all manner of other things. He was always ready, willing and, more often than not, able.

J.C. Jacobsen cared about Denmark's future, both politically and economically. He foresaw a bright future for the Danish people, and he was right: there have been ups and downs, but generally speaking the standard of living has steadily increased, as it has throughout the western world. Yet were J.C. Jacobsen able to experience Denmark today, there is no doubt that he would be searching keenly for that hard-to-define but hugely important quality which resonated with him so sonorously and inspired him in all that he did: public spirit.

All the same, this book is not an attempt to canonise the Danish industrialist who was to become the founder of one of the world's largest and best-known breweries. In human terms, J.C. Jacobsen was in many ways controversial, not least in his unswerving insistence on self-activity as an indispensable principle. There was neither rest nor quiet for the man who, in an almost manic intoxication with life, achieved the unimaginable. But the complex character of the man should not overshadow his achievements: so very few people achieve what he achieved in his lifetime. And the way in which he did it was truly remarkable.

This book has been constructed by looking back at J.C. Jacobsen's correspondences, in particular with his son Carl, but also with a number of other contemporaries, most notably the actress Johanne Louise Heiberg. It has also drawn on the many books already written about J.C. Jacobsen, the Carlsberg breweries and the Carlsberg Foundation, as well as many other books relating to Denmark's Golden Age and the nineteenth century in general.

In order to place J.C. Jacobsen and his work in an historical context, this book also touches upon the slightly wider world of the nineteenth century. Famous people with whom J.C. Jacobsen associated, or by whom he was inspired, are introduced, and crucial historical events are interwoven. This has been done to create an interaction between J.C. Jacobsen's life and the society in which he lived such that, hopefully, the book not only paints a portrait of J.C. Jacobsen but also gives an insight into an important period of Danish history.

It has not been the aim of this book to present groundbreaking new biographical material about J.C. Jacobsen: for that we have historians and other specialists. The aim has been to portray J.C. Jacobsen in a way which will hopefully be relevant for today's reader. Because there really is so much which we can learn from the man and his life.

Virum, June 2011
Anna-Lise Bjerager

CHAPTER 1: FROM CRADLE TO BREWERY

"Once upon a time" is how most fairy tales begin. And that is as good a way as any to begin the story of the brewer J.C. Jacobsen, because in so many ways his life was one long fairy tale in which the greater part of what he touched turned to gold.

J.C. Jacobsen is best known for founding and developing the Carlsberg brewery, which even in his lifetime achieved fame far beyond the borders of his native Denmark. He was a true pioneer of the brewing industry, fuelled by a vision of production based on sound craftsmanship combined with science. A vision, moreover, which he himself enacted, not least through the establishment in 1875 of the Carlsberg Laboratory, which was to make a plethora of radical discoveries in the art of brewing. So J.C. Jacobsen was not just any brewer; he was, as he has now universally become known, *the Brewer*.

And yet J.C. Jacobsen was so much more than the Brewer. J.C. Jacobsen was the socialite who understood networking long before it was actually referred to as that. His hospitality was enjoyed by many, including the famous fairy-tale writer Hans Christian Andersen, who himself was fascinated by the industrial advances of the day.

J.C. Jacobsen was the citizen who was passionate about politics and social issues, making a virtue out of working for the common good. The founding in 1876 of the Carlsberg Foundation, the world's oldest commercial foundation, ensured that the profits generated from beer largely benefited Danish society, not least through the funding of research and science.

J.C. Jacobsen was the patriot who desperately wanted to make the Danes proud once again to be Danish, particularly following the ignominious defeat and loss of territories to Prussia and Austria in 1864. He himself led the way, funding the rebuilding of the fire-ravaged Frederiksborg Castle, the pre-eminent symbol of Denmark's regal history, and setting up within its walls the Danish Museum of National History, which in 1878 was established by royal decree as an independent department of the Carlsberg Foundation.

J.C. Jacobsen was the cosmopolite who was one of just a handful of Danes to travel to the World Expo in Paris in 1878, from which he returned home triumphantly with Le Grand Prix for his beer.

J.C. Jacobsen was also, it cannot be left unsaid, the patriarch whose overcontrolling manner led him to fall out spectacularly with his only son, Carl.

Although J.C. Jacobsen was a child of his time, in many ways he was also ahead of it. Today's politicians talk a lot about cohesion in society, or, as they see it, the lack of it. Two centuries ago, J.C. Jacobsen was already addressing that very issue, determined to identify what bound people together and made them good citizens.

THE CHILDHOOD HOME J.C. Jacobsen was born in this building, where he lived with his family up to 1854. His son, Carl, was also born here. Beer was brewed here, and Old Carlsberg had its head office here until 1856. Today the building is home to the New Carlsberg Foundation, established by Carl in 1902 with the purpose of supporting the arts. (Drawing by W. Glud, 1927, from a drawing by Alfred Larsen, 1896. Carlsberg Archive)

Looking at J.C. Jacobsen and his achievements through twenty-first-century spectacles, he was also an expert in corporate social responsibility. He did not think primarily in terms of his own profit, and certainly not of shareholder value, deploring in fact the whole idea of public companies. He embraced his company with huge integrity. And on behalf of the company he assumed great responsibility for his employees and the surrounding community, demonstrated not least in his extensive patronages.

Throughout his lifetime J.C. Jacobsen was indefatigable in all that he undertook. "I'm not cut out for pottering around," he wrote to Carl. He certainly wasn't! He worked voraciously from early in the morning till late at night right up to his death in Rome in 1887.

Humble beginnings

Although J.C. Jacobsen's life presents itself as one long success story, it began humbly enough in a Copenhagen apartment.

J.C. Jacobsen was born on 2 September 1811 in the heart of Copenhagen, which had known brewhouses since the 1600s. His parents were Christen Jacobsen, a copyhold farmer's son drawn to the capital to try his luck at brewing, and Caroline Frederikke Schelbeck, the daughter of a Copenhagen silk weaver.

On the day of J.C. Jacobsen's birth all was seemingly quiet in Copenhagen. At any rate, the leading metropolitan newspaper of the day had no big news to report: the author and poet Bernhard Severin Ingemann, of whom J.C. Jacobsen was to become a fan, had published his first collection of poems, and six men had scaled Mont Blanc. There was also the latest news from Christiania (present-day Oslo) in Norway, which was still part of the Kingdom of Denmark.

Perhaps everything oozed peace and quiet in the newspaper's columns because at that time Denmark was still subject to absolute monarchy as a form of government. King Frederik VI, who reigned from 1808 to 1839, may have been loved by the Danish people, but he was no great supporter of the new ideas and political currents which characterised the age, and censorship was the order of the day. The king was keen to prevent what he referred to as "editorial impudence".

Having said that, the inhabitants of Copenhagen were very much in need of a period of respite because the preceding years had been wretched. War had raged in Europe, and Denmark had become unwittingly embroiled in the conflict between Britain and France.

Britain wanted to deny Napoleon further power, and in an attempt to stop Danish ships carrying goods in and out of French ports, the British fleet sailed to Copenhagen, culminating in the Battle of Copenhagen in 1801. Six years later the British returned, this time to prevent Napoleon from seizing the Danish fleet. This was achieved with the bombardment of Copenhagen, which led to the Danish surrender.

The wars with the British left Denmark bankrupt. At the same time, the Treaty of Kiel in 1814, which ended Danish participation in the Napoleonic Wars, forced Denmark to relinquish Norway to Sweden, severing a union which had lasted since 1397.

Denmark's Golden Age

The bombardment of Copenhagen took place just four years before J.C. Jacobsen was born, and it would undoubtedly have been a regular topic of conversation in his childhood.

Close to their home the family could see first-hand the damage caused by the British attack. The Church of Our Lady,

THE BOMBARDMENT OF COPENHAGEN The bombardment of Copenhagen, which was the first ever terror attack on a civilian population, destroyed three hundred homes and killed a large number of civilians, estimated variously at between two hundred and three thousand.

The British troops, who demanded the surrender of the Danish fleet as part of the Napoleonic Wars, instigated the battle on 16 August 1807 by going ashore at Vedbæk north of Copenhagen.

On 1 and 2 September the British invited the Danish general to surrender the Danish fleet. The invitation was declined.

The bombardment took place between 2 and 5 September. Incendiary rockets were used until eventually the houses which remained were empty of residents and the local fire defence had disintegrated.

On 6 September the Danish surrendered. Denmark was compelled to relinquish its fleet, and the British destroyed the fleet's stores on Holmen and elsewhere. Denmark was thus forced to abandon its neutrality and take the side of France in the Napoleonic Wars.

The painter C.W. Eckersberg immortalised the moment when the spire of the Church of Our Lady was hit and burst into flames. The church subsequently burnt to the ground. (*The Tower of the Church of Our Lady on Fire*, colour lithography by G.I. Lahde, from C.W. Eckersberg's painting of the bombardment of Copenhagen on the night of 5 September 1807. Museum of Copenhagen)

which was situated on a nearby street boasting no less than twenty-four of the one hundred brewhouses in the city, was among the buildings destroyed.

All the same, when Christen and Caroline Jacobsen carried their first and – as it would turn out – only child the short distance to the Helliggeist Church (situated in what is today Copenhagen's pedestrian shopping street, Strøget) for the joyous occasion of the christening, the situation of their country was probably not on their minds. The godparents were the parents themselves and, in keeping with custom, the midwife. As she had helped the child into the world, she also had a part to play in its future, or so the reasoning went.

The child was named Jacob Christian Jacobsen. In later years he would always sign his name J.C. Jacobsen and liked to refer to himself as Captain from his rank in the Civic Guard, which was made up of several military bodies in Copenhagen.

Perhaps on their way to the church the small family passed some of Copenhagen's glitterati of the day. The sculptor Bertel Thorvaldsen was residing in Rome, but from time to time he still visited Copenhagen. The author and hymn writer Nikolaj Frederik Severin Grundtvig and the aforementioned B.S. Ingemann called the capital their home. So too the poet and playwright Adam Oehlenschläger. Most of these were people whom J.C. Jacobsen would come to admire in his adult life.

Some years later, the philosopher Søren Kierkegaard, who was born two years after J.C. Jacobsen, would eagerly walk the same streets of inner Copenhagen. "I have walked myself into my best thoughts," he once observed.

The artists Christen Købke, Christoffer Wilhelm Eckersberg and Johan Thomas Lundbye also dwelt in the Danish capital, as did the celebrated brothers Anders Sandoe Oersted and Hans Christian Oersted. The latter's ideas and work in the fields of chemistry and physics would later be a source of fascination for J.C. Jacobsen.

These were all people of intellect and wit whose thinking went beyond the borders of Denmark. Perhaps because, in spite of the loss of Norway in 1814, Denmark was still at this time a big country, there was room for big ideas, even if it could be a little cramped within the ramparts of the overpopulated Copenhagen, which was home to around a hundred thousand people.

Paradoxically, it seems that even though there was a lot wrong politically and economically, the cultural scene was blossoming. The period from 1802 to 1850 is known as Denmark's Golden Age, and this too was part of the reality into which J.C. Jacobsen was born, albeit a journeyman brewer like his father, even though he had been promoted upon the birth of his son to tenant brewer, still did not belong to the class of society upon

THE KING'S BREWHOUSE (KONGENS BRYGHUS) Christen Jacobsen, who
had been taken on as a brewery hand at The King's Brewhouse, slowly worked
his way up. At the time when he was elected a director of the board of The King's
Brewhouse, he was also in the process of establishing his own brewery. (Drawing by
Alfred Larsen, 1915. Carlsberg Archive)

which most gold was sprinkled. Having obtained a licence, a tenant brewer was able to rent the brewhouse from the owner. Brewhouse owners included among their number admirals and priests, and even the Church of Our Lady had its own brewhouse.

A brewing apprenticeship

As the young Jacob Christian grew up, things slowly improved for his father Christen, who had a good head for both brewing and money.

Industrialisation had not yet fully established itself in Denmark, but Christen loved all the new things that began to appear, and he was ambitious.

It was in these years that the old brewers' guilds were abolished and brewing became a free trade which could be practised by anyone, assuming of course that they had taken out a licence to trade. This meant that a person had been granted royal assent to conduct business in the city. Only then was the person considered to be a citizen in the legal sense.

Over the next fifteen years Christen Jacobsen acquired both a licence to trade and a brewery. He became a co-owner of The King's Brewhouse, the oldest brewery in Denmark, and also one of three board directors.

The small family had become part of the growing middle class between the nobility and the peasantry, and with it came certain obligations. That at least is how it must have felt for a copyhold farmer's son who had made it all the way to the capital solely by virtue of the will of the Lord, a meagre village schooling, a good head on his shoulders, and no small measure of talent. But it would not do to rest on his laurels. He had to fight to progress even further. And it was important that he should pass on the fight to his son, who needed to work hard at his studies and at the craft of brewing.

THE CHILDHOOD LOCALITY The bustling Højbro Square was situated not far from J.C. Jacobsen's home and close to his school. Most of the buildings shown are still standing. (*View of Højbro Square*, painting by Sally Henriques, 1844. © SMK Foto. National Gallery of Denmark, Copenhagen)

Christen was determined that his son should get educated. But, on the other hand, it was essential that he should temper his eagerness for education. After all, he was not to be a scholar, but a brewer like his father.

The young Jacob Christian wanted it all. He was bright and inquisitive, and he received top grades in school. But at the age of fourteen he finished school to take up an apprenticeship in brewing. He still kept up his learning, partly by attending lectures given by H.C. Oersted at the College of Advanced Technology, now the Technical University of Denmark. His father also attended, and was inspired, among other things, to become one of the first brewers to use a thermometer in the brewing process. At that time, most brewers made do with sticking a finger into the brew and guessing the temperature.

The encounter with science was of crucial importance for both father and son. They heard Professor Oersted say that nothing happened without a reason. But how could this be brought to bear on the fermentation of beer, for example, where no one had any idea why the beer could turn bad just a few days after having been good? Both father and son understood that the world of science might benefit them enormously if only they could understand it better.

An out-and-out Romantic

At the same time, the younger brewer also understood that there were lots of other worlds to study. He read and perfected his knowledge within a number of areas. Mathematics, Antiquity and German literature were among his favourite subjects, and he loved reading the works of the Danish Romantic writers such as Adam Oehlenschläger, B.S. Ingemann and Johan Ludvig Heiberg, whom in later life he was apt to quote at great length. At a young age J.C. Jacobsen was already an out-and-out Romantic.

When J.C. Jacobsen had turned 23, a young merchant's daughter from Jutland came to stay with the Jacobsen family. Her name was Laura Holst. Later on she would become the permanent lady of the house. In the first instance, Laura brought new life to the home through her family. Her brother-in-law was a doctor, Frants Djørup, who would become J.C. Jacobsen's closest friend throughout his lifetime. Student friends of Frants

Djørup from Jutland also visited, becoming part of the social circle and engaging in lively discussion wherever they went.

The "brewing chap", as they called J.C. Jacobsen, could actually be rather quiet. But they were all impressed at his intelligence in pretty much every area. One day a group of students and J.C. Jacobsen visited an art exhibition at the Charlottenborg Exhibition Hall. It was no surprise that it was the brewing chap who guided the group from work to work.

The fact that J.C. Jacobsen never pursued his formal education further gave him a certain lifelong feeling of inferiority which does not seem to have been justified. As Frants Djørup said of him: "We were impressed at his wealth of knowledge, concise logic in discussion and diverse interests." And, given his upbringing, this was maybe not all that unexpected. When his father Christen died in 1835 at the age of sixty-two, the same Frants Djørup eulogised that he was "a remarkably gifted person, perhaps even more gifted than his son".

At that time, the wind of change was gusting through the brewing industry in Denmark. Up to then, brewers had been producing "white" beer of a somewhat dubious nature. But now there was a new beer in town: from Bavaria in Germany, this was bottom-fermented lager beer with a very different taste, and it rather appealed to the Copenhagen taste buds. J.C. Jacobsen was now the sole Brewer Jacobsen. The challenge was his to meet. The time of *the Brewer* had come.

Yeast in a hatbox

One day the Brewer and Frants Djørup were walking past a wine merchant's in the centre of Copenhagen which was serving Bavarian beer. Somewhat warily the Brewer ordered a glass of the dark, sharp-tasting lager beer. Djørup ventured a sip of the beer but didn't care much for the flavour, but the Brewer took

SPACE FOR BEER There was space for seven hundred barrels of beer in the newly acquired storage cellar in Hahns Bastion. This space would be needed because in November 1845 J.C. Jacobsen returned from Munich with yeast for the production of his first bottom-fermented beer. That winter he brewed three hundred barrels of Bavarian beer. (Drawing by T. Bøgelund, undated. Carlsberg Archive)

an extra gulp and declared that it definitely warranted further investigation.

The Brewer believed with his usual fervour that it simply had to be possible to emulate the Germans, and he immediately set off for Hamburg to find out more about the production method behind the bottom-fermented lager beer.

When he returned home, he conducted his first trial. No doubt to keep his cards close to his chest in regard to a trial for which he could not guarantee the outcome, the brewing of the new Bavarian beer did not take place in the actual brewery, but in the cellar of his home. And, what is more, in his mother's copper, which is still in the possession of the brewery today. It is said that the first Danish-produced Bavarian beer was brewed in that copper, but, alas, that is not true because Bavarian beer was already being brewed by Thomas Charles Grut in Odense in 1834.

Myths have a habit of attaching themselves to the Brewer. What is certain, however, is that in 1845 he travelled to Munich to visit the Zum Späten brewery and the legendary brewer Gabriel Sedlmayr, and from there he brought back a bottom-fermenting yeast which for many years provided the strain for Carlsberg's beer production.

Transporting yeast, which is after all a living organism, from Munich to Copenhagen may seem easy today. But back then, before planes and railways, the only real means of transport available to the Brewer was the stagecoach, a covered wagon with two horses harnessed up for carrying people and small packages.

One can imagine the Brewer inside the stagecoach on his way back from Munich, squeezed between the other passengers and their packages, with a hatbox on his knee. At the bottom of the hatbox was a tin containing the precious yeast, which had to be kept cool to prevent it from fermenting. Every time the stagecoach made a stop, whether day or night, the Brewer rushed to the nearest water pump to pour cold water over the tin. Eventually the yeast arrived safely in Copenhagen.

In May 1846 various beer merchants advertised a Bavarian beer from "Brewer Jacobsen's cellar under the ramparts". A full bottle sold for four times the price of a loaf of rye bread.

A brewing dynasty in its infancy

Life, as they say, is more than beer and skittles. And even though the Brewer busied himself day and night working out how he could take his brewery forward, he understood the importance of starting a family. In 1839 he had married Laura Holst, the merchant's daughter from Jutland. He took pleasure in both her and her family. And she for her part loved him her whole life. Today we would say that through the course of the marriage they grew apart, but they retained a mutual fondness for one another their entire lives, as evidenced by several letters.

On 2 March 1842 Laura gave the Brewer a son, Carl, who would go on to brew beer just like his father. After Carl was born, the Brewer began thinking of moving his brewery. Copenhagen had become too cramped for him. When his mother died in 1844, leaving him a sizeable inheritance, he began looking for a suitable plot of land outside the city ramparts with space for storage cellars and, essential for the brewing process, clean water, which was a scarce commodity in Copenhagen.

Once again it was Frants Djørup who had to lend an ear to his plans. The Brewer took his friend to Valby, at that time an independent village outside Copenhagen, where they trudged around on a bitingly cold spring day. Near Valby Hill digging was under way for the new railway line which would connect Copenhagen and Roskilde. As the Brewer questioned the workers and tested the quality of the soil, he was apparently completely unaffected by the weather. Djørup, by contrast, remembers feeling miserably cold.

When the Brewer later established that there was lots of water in Valby Hill, he was ready to apply to the king for permission to build and run a Bavarian beer brewery and storage cellars on the outskirts of Copenhagen. When permission was granted, he bought about four acres of land in Valby. He sought a not insubstantial loan (around four times what he had inherited) from a commercial firm, which was certainly no straight-

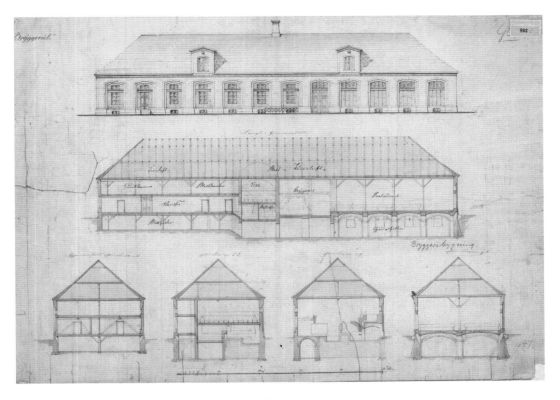

THE FIRST CARLSBERG In 1847 J.C. Jacobsen himself drew the basic sketches
for his new brewery in Valby. (Carlsberg Archive)

forward matter as there was still a good deal of scepticism at
industrial building in Denmark. Yet he succeeded.

On a spring day in 1847 building work began on the Carlsberg brewery which we know today. When the topping-out
ceremony took place, the Brewer chose to pour, not beer, but
wine over a chimney in the middle of the site. The brewery was
named Carlsberg, combining the name of his then five-year-old
son with "bjerg", meaning "mountain", a tongue-in-cheek reference to Valby Hill.

The Brewer's lifelong project had entered its opening phase.

CHAPTER 2:
THE PATRIARCH

When Carl reached the age of thirteen, he received a watch from his father accompanied by a letter which read:

"My dear Carl! If you had been a really good, hard-working boy in the past year, this watch would have become yours today. I cannot give it to you now, though, because you have not earned it. I hope, however, that you will do your best to earn it. I will therefore lend it to you to look at and be regulated by in your room, but you may not wear it until you have once again achieved the position in class that you had before. Your loving father Jacobsen."

The year was 1855. In the previous year the family had moved out to Valby, where the Brewer had built a grand home for his small family next to the Carlsberg brewery. The Brewer had been assisted by architects and other specialists, but he himself had drawn the basic sketches for the buildings and the heating and ventilation systems. He was rightly proud of his work, which was being elaborated for the next thirty years. Painstaking, as with all the other projects which he would undertake later in his life, the Brewer was also keen in this venture to contrive something really big.

The Brewer had a dream that his home would become a gathering place for a select band of erudite men and women from the worlds of art and science. And indeed, after his death the main building went on to be an honorary residence for, among others, the philosopher Harald Høffding and the atomic physicist Niels Bohr. In 1997 the house was turned into the Carlsberg Academy and is used for scientific symposia and meetings.

The Brewer began with the garden: aided by a gardener, in 1848-49 he established a park. His many trips inspired him to buy rare plants and trees, and with the soil from the excavated beer cellars he created a rolling landscape. The main building was built between 1851 and 1855, and in 1858 the winter garden was established. In 1876 the Brewer built his greenhouse, which he called "Pompeii" because its columns brought to mind the ancient Italian city, which the Brewer had visited with Carl.

The focal point of the main building, which the Brewer spent many years ornamenting, was the Captain's Room, where Wilhelm Marstrand's portrait of H.C. Oersted hung on the wall together with Michelangelo's prophets and sibyls. The ceiling in the dining hall was nine metres high and adorned with the works of the sculptor Bertel Thorvaldsen. On the terrace leading out to the landscaped garden stood the Venus de Milo, and from the Italian pergola one could see in the evening the lighthouse on top of Stevns Cliff, some forty kilometres away.

As the Brewer told his young son: "I have built this house,

THE CARLSBERG ACADEMY The Brewer's home has been converted into the Carlsberg Academy, which is used today for symposia and meetings. (Carlsberg Archive)

Carl, not to have a magnificent building for my residence, but in order to make something beautiful." In all truth, it was probably a combination of the two.

So here, in this impressive home, one imagines Carl sitting in his room reading the birthday letter from his father.

Carl was a talented and clever boy, but "a bit of a slow learner", as he himself later recalled. Furthermore, he had a stammer. This might easily be explained by the huge weight of expectation placed upon him. No good results in school, no

THE CAPTAIN'S ROOM The Brewer oversaw all manner of things from his desk in his office at Old Carlsberg, which was called the Captain's Room. From here he had a view of the brewery. Here too was the drawing board which he used studiously for his many technical and architectural creations. (Carlsberg Archive)

LAURA'S ROOM Laura's Room was decorated by the Brewer and looked out over the winter garden. (Carlsberg Archive)

watch. Harsh maybe, but for the Brewer there was a lot at stake. It was fully in keeping with his own view when Frants Djørup had stood up at the moving-in party at Carlsberg and toasted Carl as "Jacobsen's best hope".

Fighting spirit prevails

Eight years had passed since work had begun on the brewery, and the Brewer had overcome a great deal of adversity getting the brewery on its feet. Disastrously, the well that was to supply water for production had run dry. At that time, the Brewer had genuinely feared that he was a ruined man. Walking home alongside the new railway line to Laura and Carl in the inner city, on more than one occasion he considered throwing himself in front of the train and ending it all. But his fighting spirit prevailed. The water problem was solved and the brewery was back on track.

The new railways had made the world smaller, and in those years he had also travelled extensively, making numerous trips to Germany, Austria, Belgium, France and England to share experiences with brewers and soak up new knowledge. In 1851 he was even accompanied by Laura and Carl on a tour of northern Italy and Germany.

The Brewer maintained his political commitments, which had started back in 1843 when he became a member of the Copenhagen City Council. He had also become part of Danish high society. Carlsberg was visited by many of the leading politicians and scientists of the day, and every Friday the Brewer kept an open house, where a core of close friends would be joined by new acquaintances. One regular attendee, Professor Rasmus Nielsen, observed when the candelabra had been lit and Thorvaldsen's sculptures lined the table: "The gods are seated for dinner."

J.C. Jacobsen, 1846. (Carlsberg Archive)
Laura Jacobsen, ca 1850. (Carlsberg Archive)
Carl Jacobsen, 1852. (Carlsberg Archive)

Many years later Carl remembered how under no circumstances would his father brook compliments or witticism at the table: "My father was a decidedly serious man." He also recalled that Hans Christian Andersen would read his fairy tales aloud, and that the actor and opera singer Peter Jerndorff would sing "with so much emotion that our eyes misted over". On a day-to-day basis, however, life at Carlsberg was almost spartan.

This is not as paradoxical as it sounds. It was not long since the Brewer's father had arrived empty-handed from the farm in rural Jutland. The difficult times were still fresh in the memory. But the fact remained that the Brewer had done better than well. His hard work had borne fruit.

A master in the home

Now it was a matter of educating his son, who would continue his magnum opus: the brewery. This task the Brewer took upon himself as if his very life depended on it, which is why Carl was sitting in his room with a watch which he was not permitted to wear until such time as he had earned the right to do so. Yet even when Carl had grown up and left home, he remained subject to the tyranny of his father's love.

The word "patriarch" comes from the Greek "pater" (father) plus "archon" (ruler). Ruler over a family, one might add. The Brewer was such a ruler. Not only over his family, and in particular his only son, but also over his employees at Carlsberg and others for whom he felt a responsibility. Patriarchies, where men rule in the family and in society in general, are the norm in the world and have been since time immemorial.

Since the end of the nineteenth century the patriarchal model has been challenged in the western world, not least by women's movements. For her part, though, Laura was very much a woman of her time and wanted nothing to do with feminine revolt. She was shaped by the old social norms. Later in life she visited the Royal Theatre in Copenhagen with her husband to watch a performance of Henrik Ibsen's *A Doll's House*. Neither she nor the Brewer cared much for the rebellious character of Nora, who breaks free of her marriage. "The young women of today want to be pampered, they want men to acquiesce in every little thing," she wrote to a friend. "Jacobsen naturally agrees with me in assessing *A Doll's House*. He will not have it said that he pampered his wife or gave her too much independence."

Laura is described as gentle and devout, and as the lady of the house who governed with authority indoors. But she was not always allowed to do so by her over-zealous husband, who also wanted his say in household affairs, and it was when it came to parties at Carlsberg that the Brewer was most wont to interfere.

Not quite perfect

Evidence that the Brewer was not always the perfect husband is to be found in the letters of the young girl Nanna, who was a distant relation from Jutland and the companion-help for Laura from 1863 to 1866.

"Uncle's unreasonableness and pitilessness engender in Auntie a subdued and meek disposition – at times her jealously also breaks out, and not always without reason."

It was not that the Brewer was unfaithful to his wife. But throughout his life he enjoyed the company of intelligent women who possessed personality and wit. His long-term friendship with the actress Johanne Louise Heiberg, with whom he conducted a keen correspondence, was a perfect example of this, as were his horseback rides in the countryside around Carlsberg with the young Emmy Moltke, another of his circle of acquaintances. The Brewer also inclined to a certain male vanity; if he were due to go riding with Emmy Moltke, he liked to put in some training beforehand.

When the French scientist Louis Pasteur visited Copenhagen in 1884 for the International Medical Congress, a party was held at Carlsberg. At that time Laura was visiting a health resort abroad and so was not present at the festivities. Some days beforehand the Brewer had his carriage prepared and drove into town on an urgent errand with the wife of Søren Anton van der Aa Kühle, the technical director of Carlsberg. The errand? Mrs van der Aa Kühle was to be provided with a new party outfit, and the choice fell to a green brocade dress, as recounted in the memoirs of her daughter Ingeborg Schmidt.

Such favours were rarely bestowed upon Laura. Nevertheless, the Brewer was in all ways considerate towards his wife, and always mindful that Carl should be kind to his mother. "Buy something for your mother. I dare say she could use a shawl," he wrote to Carl, who was abroad at the time.

When he himself gave gifts to Laura, they were often of a practical nature. In a letter to Laura on the occasion of her sixty-seventh birthday in 1886, he wrote: "Tomorrow you will receive from Cathrine a parcel, which is a birthday present from me. It contains 3 pairs of lace curtains for the garden room in the same style as the old ones, which are no longer fit for purpose. As such curtains cannot now be obtained on the market, I inquired through Bertha whether Ottilia [Carl's wife, ed.] in Edinburgh might look out for replicas, in which, as you shall see, she succeeded. They may not be precisely the same pattern, but they are just as beautiful. Please therefore thank her from me. Yours devotedly, J.C. Jacobsen."

The fact is that the Brewer's relationship with women seems somewhat confused. At one point he enthuses with Carl

THE BREWER AND HIS EMPLOYEES From the very beginning the Brewer took on young men from the farming class with strong physiques. It was tough work handling the heavy casks, and many of the workers sustained back injuries. It was an advantage if job candidates had done military service as this guaranteed a certain amount of discipline. (Photograph of J.C. Jacobsen and his employees, 1885. Carlsberg Archive)

about "some day finding a strong, true love for a noble woman of such esteem that one might approach with humility, feel respect. A woman whom one would not for anything in the world show inconsiderateness and selfishness, whom one should be afraid to lose."

The Brewer probably never met such a woman himself, and the question remains whether she was merely a product of his own imagination.

A father figure in the workplace

When it came to Carlsberg, the Brewer was a strong father figure. The workers who were not married lived at the brewery and were watched carefully. They had to observe a ten o'clock curfew, and they had to be sober. If they broke the rules, they were fined according to an intricate system and the indiscretions were recorded in the inspector's notebook, which contained entries such as: "N.P. Petersen went out without permission, fined 1 krone"; "Peter Frederiksen asleep during working hours, fined 1 krone"; "Kiertinge fined 5 kroner for throwing a full cask of beer at Jens Clemmensen"; and "A.P. Nielsen fined 10 kroner because he could not be roused in the morning." However, the fines were not to be paid to the Brewer. The workers were required to go down to a shelter for the poor, pay their fine and bring back a receipt.

Up until 1860 the bachelors were catered for by Laura Jacobsen, who drew up a menu and provided a good, varied diet. They ate with the coachman, the matron, the cook and the maid in the basement, and mealtimes were announced by the ringing of a bell, as opposed to the horn which was blown upstairs in the dining hall for the Brewer and his family.

The bachelors and other fixed-wage staff received their pay in gold once a month and enjoyed the best conditions. They worked in production in the brewery, in the yeast cellars and malthouse, in racking off and in cleaning casks. They had their own "servants' hall", where they ate their food after Laura Jacobsen stopped catering for them, and they were given beer to drink during the day.

One bachelor recalls how many of them became experts in cooking meals such as chicken soup.

"When there were a few of us who got together to make this sort of dish, we had a great evening. We also had a reading room where newspapers and books were provided for us. And a bowling alley, although that could only be used in the summer as it wasn't under cover. It was situated between the red warehouse and the pitch shed. Yep, we had some great times as bachelors."

The day labourers, who were paid in paper money once a week, did not enjoy the same conditions. They had to clean the cellars, do painting and various washing duties, polish harnesses, and help out in the cellars. They also had to sweep and roll the roads and clear snow in the winter. They were not given any beer, and they had no access to the servants' hall but sat around in the brewery wherever they could find a space.

It is worth noting, however, that although the Brewer was a strict employer, he took many steps to exercise modern management, for example introducing an advanced recruitment and pay system to promote quality in beer production as much as possible. If they applied themselves, employees had an opportunity to advance and learn new things.

A sacred duty

The Brewer believed in many ways that work was a sacred duty, and this was a view that he communicated to those around him. When Carl grew older and, in his father's opinion, became too generous with his patronage, the Brewer set him straight:

"'In the sweat of thy face shalt thou eat bread.' This is God's message for mankind's own good. Only then will you enjoy the good things in life as a fruit of your labour," he wrote, quoting the book of Genesis in the Old Testament.

But at the same time the Brewer was also indirectly influenced by the Lutheran doctrine of vocation and profession:

"Your work is a very sacred matter. God delights in it, and through it he wants to bestow his blessing on you," wrote Martin Luther. Thinking which the Brewer undoubtedly encountered both in the home and in catechistic teaching at school.

Luther believed that man had to work to be useful. One should not work for one's own sake, but to serve one's neighbour. And is it not in the interest of one's neighbour when the shoemaker makes shoes and the baker bakes bread? Lutheranism upgrades work as a phenomenon by emphasising its usefulness. And it was usefulness which preoccupied the Brewer.

The companion-help Nanna wrote: "I find it sad to hear someone [the Brewer, ed.] who would seem to have every prospect of success, joy and pleasure in life say that it is usefulness which must be derived from all things. There is no pleasure in such a life."

The Brewer worked constantly and believed that every single minute of the day, unless one was sleeping, should be spent being useful.

The perfectionist

At the same time, the Brewer was what today we would call a perfectionist. As a child, for example, he found drawing and writing difficult. Most people would reason that there was probably something else they were good at and concentrate on that. But in the Brewer's case it was quite the opposite. The tougher the battle, the harder he fought. And the Brewer was a natural fighter. The fact that he found drawing and writing so difficult meant that he made an extra effort in these particular areas. And this bore fruit: the Brewer became an accomplished self-taught architect as an adult and developed a handwriting which, in the view of Johanne Louise Heiberg, was the "most agreeable" gentleman's handwriting with which she had ever become acquainted.

At the age of seventy-four the Brewer reaffirmed his

lifelong love of perfection and of work: "I have never found an affinity with size, but only with perfection, and consequently I have had an innate drive, supported by an equally innate satisfaction in work, which for me has been and remains the sweetest pleasure," he wrote to Johanne Louise Heiberg.

So what was the driving force behind the huge work effort which the Brewer manifested throughout his lifetime?

A psychologist today would perhaps begin by assuming that this almost manic desire for perfection and ceaseless endeavour must surely mask repression on a large scale. Suffice to say, perhaps, that here too the Brewer showed the way – albeit not necessarily in a particularly heroic way. Today many people find it difficult leaving their work behind them at the end of the day, and we speak of "workaholics" without it being entirely clear whether the term is meant positively or negatively. It is not unusual today for both the boss and the secretary to "go down with stress", to use the modern parlance. The Brewer did not suffer from stress. He was far too controlled for that. Control which he not only exercised over himself, but also over others, not least Carl.

Nowadays we would refer to the Brewer as a classic pattern-breaker on his way up the social ladder. That is not always an easy role to fill, and it would seem that the Brewer never felt fully at home in the social milieux in which he moved throughout his life.

The pattern-breaker

As a young man who had left school at an early age, the Brewer felt inferior in the company of students who had completed their schooling. Having attained prosperity, he invited people to parties, but one does not get the feeling that he really felt the equal of his guests. Even though he was highly respected as a

BEER FOR HANS CHRISTIAN ANDERSEN The writer Hans Christian Andersen (1805-1875) achieved international renown in his own lifetime as one of the most original authors of the nineteenth century. In particular, his fairy tales such as *The Tinder Box*, *The Ugly Duckling*, *The Snow Queen* and *The Princess and the Pea* have gone from strength to strength.

The Brewer was a contemporary of Hans Christian Andersen and often invited him to Carlsberg for dinner as well as providing for him in other ways. Hans Christian Andersen wrote in his diary entry for 18 October 1874:

"…at home I received a letter from Brewer Jacobsen saying that yesterday he had sent me 12 half-bottles of Export and that throughout the winter I should satisfy my needs from his cellar until such time came as this type of beer were once again available on the market." (*Portrait of Hans Christian Andersen*, painting by C.A. Jensen, 1836. Odense City Museums)

brewer and as a citizen, and despite being always certain and forthright in his behaviour, he did not necessarily have great self-esteem. Rather, perhaps, a certain unrecognised inferiority and the pattern-breaker's constant awareness that this is a world into which one was not born. One has only been granted admittance having first worked oneself to the bone.

This interpretation can be tentatively drawn, partly from a letter which the Brewer wrote to Carl following a dinner party at Carlsberg in 1866. The guests were members of the Rigsdag (the Danish Parliament) and of the Defence Commission, of which the Brewer was chairman.

"I regard it as one of the most delicious fruits of my endeavour and my good fortune to be able to gather such a circle around me. I cannot but gladly compare my position and intellectual standing now with those which I occupied when I was walking about in wooden shoes, washing casks at home in the yard and driving the brewery wagon around to the alehouses: and even later – much, much later – when I felt so shy and bashful towards anyone whom I did not know well and when my horizon was so limited that I could not concern myself with anything but brewing, a little chemistry and physics, and a dash of aesthetics. How could I at that time dream that I should come to preside at my own table over such a circle of men as I saw there yesterday?"

It sounds not unlike a retelling of Hans Christian Andersen's *Ugly Duckling*, which is the fairy-tale writer's parable of his own pattern-breaking ascent from poverty and hardship to world fame. The fairy tale ends with the sentence: "I never dreamed of so much happiness when I was the ugly duckling!"

Whereas, however, Hans Christian Andersen sought world fame as a writer, the Brewer sought social recognition. And now these distinguished guests were sitting in his drawing room, their mere presence a token of how far he had come. This social striving, combined with a ceaseless striving for perfection in both his personal and working lives, was presumably a strong driving force for the Brewer.

Entrepreneur and coach

The Brewer, who wanted to do everything himself, naturally also wanted to head up the management of the brewery. But after falling ill with rheumatic fever in 1849 and being laid up for some time, he saw the need to appoint an inspector. Over the years a number of inspectors were taken on to work with the Brewer on the day-to-day management.

Erhard Kogsbølle, who filled the position from 1856 to 1881, after which he went on to found his own brewery, was the inspector who remained at Carlsberg the longest. He was also the Brewer's partner from 1871 to 1881, which meant that in this period the company changed its name to J.C. Jacobsen & Co. Kogsbølle was especially skilled in the arts of box malting and steam cooking, as well as being on very close terms with the Brewer. So close in fact that the Brewer hosted his wedding and built a home at Carlsberg for the Kogsbølle family.

In this day and age such a close relationship between owner and administrative manager would set corporate governance whistles blowing, but at the time both corporate form and thinking were rather different.

The Brewer regarded his brewery as a brewing school where a person could work for a short or long period before starting out independently. "My brewery should be a breeding ground for young brewers," he declared.

When August Vogelius, Erhard Kogsbølle's predecessor as inspector at Carlsberg, had left the company, the Brewer had been more than happy to help out. Vogelius had taken out a tenancy on the Brewer's old white-beer brewery in the centre of Copenhagen, but as the equipment was rather outdated, the Brewer decided after a few years to knock it down and instead helped Vogelius to acquire his own brewery. The Brewer designed the brewery himself and took charge of fitting it out.

In this, as in other areas, the Brewer seems to be something of a paradox. On the one hand, he represents the old world with its orthodoxy and order, expecting obedience and loyalty from his employees. On the other hand, he is the herald of a new age redolent of the entrepreneurship and coaching of our own times.

It is a defining characteristic of modern society that all authority is vulnerable. This was not the case in the Brewer's time, which was before psychoanalysis and the emancipation of women, and before Nietzsche proclaimed that God is dead. It was before modernity. So it is important to remember, in the face of a temptation to be outraged by the Brewer and to construe him as tyrannical and non-pedagogical, that he should be judged against the norms and values of his own time. He was out of the ordinary in many ways. But as a husband, father and employer who exercised the authority which had been handed down to him by his own father, he was also in many other ways rather ordinary.

Carl receives his mentoring

Nevertheless, it is interesting to dwell a while on the Brewer's relationship with Carl because it was so important for the further development of Carlsberg. That relationship is illuminated first and foremost by the many letters which the Brewer wrote to Carl over the years (Carl's letters have, unfortunately, mostly been lost) and letters from the young girl whom we have already met, Nanna.

The Brewer kept a strict watch over his son's schooling. Carl attended Borgerdydskolen ("the School of Civic Virtue", dedicated to educating the broader public) in Copenhagen. When the family had moved to Valby, it meant that Carl had a long way to go to school, but he attended faithfully. The Brewer made sure that his son gained an insight into history and journeyed with him in southern Jutland and Schleswig during the summer holidays. He also attached importance to providing him with an appreciation of art and took him along to galleries, museums and the theatre.

Generally speaking, mentoring was an important part of everyday life for Carl. As he was still having problems with his stammer at the age of seventeen, the Brewer decided that he should go on a trip to Switzerland and Paris accompanied by a teacher who could work on his speech defect. The trip was planned in advance down to the finest detail by the Brewer. Carl was given a diary, in which his father had noted any practical information, and his father had helped pack socks, shirts and undergarments for the trip. Throughout his entire life the Brewer was unable to relax this endless instruction and mollycoddling of his son.

In 1861, at the instigation of his father Carl began attending lectures in chemistry and physics at the Royal Veterinary and Agricultural University and at the College of Advanced

Technology, where he subsequently became a student. Carl was to receive more technical and theoretical brewing training than the Brewer himself.

In the middle of his studies, however, Carl fell in love. The woman in question was Emilie Djørup, Frants Djørup's niece, whom he courted in secret for some years. His father was opposed to the relationship, but the young couple continued their courtship all the same. "It is amusing to hear how they, Carl and Emilie, lead the old people a merry dance," wrote Nanna, who was a confidante of both young lovers and soon discovered that they wished to become engaged.

The Brewer was in a state of high alert. He did not believe that his son was mature enough to get engaged, young as he was and with no qualifications. At the same time, the Brewer was also of the conviction that his son had a form of character defect, which he was not unwilling to see as his own fault, admitting that his son had not been accustomed to strict, respectful conditions in the parental home. Furthermore, the Brewer was not taken with Carl's would-be fiancée. He believed that Emilie had many of the same weaknesses as his son, and that the young couple therefore made a poor match.

Exile

One April evening in 1866 the Brewer set his twenty-four-year-old son on board a steamship bound for Lübeck in Germany, from where he would continue on to Paris. The Brewer was intransigent: by hook or by crook Carl needed to be distanced from his infatuation and from home if he were to truly grow up. The Brewer was stubbornly resolved to mould Carl in his own image, and in the coming years he wrote a number of letters full of admonishment and advice with this purpose in mind.

Four years were to pass before Carl returned home. In the

first two years, he studied and visited French and German breweries. In the next two, he spent his time similarly in Scotland and England. Carl was never asked, but there is actually nothing to suggest that he openly rebelled against his father at this time.

On that evening at the quayside, however, and later back at home at Carlsberg, the Brewer was hit by the separation from his son which he himself had brought about. "I regularly have a crushing feeling of emptiness, which often brings tears to my eyes," he wrote to Carl shortly after his departure. "It is worst on those frequent occasions when I look into your room, and yet I cannot stop myself from visiting it."

A year after Carl's departure, disaster struck at Carlsberg. Early in the morning of 6 April 1867 a fire broke out. In just a few hours the fire spread from the ceiling above the steam boiler, where the workers had thrown their wet clothes to dry and presumably a pipe or cigarette butt had been forgotten. The Brewer himself took part in the efforts to fight the fire, but it was all in vain. By eight o'clock in the morning the brewery had burnt to the ground. Fortunately, the brewery's warehouses, containing full casks of beer, were intact, and sales for the summer were secure. Although the Brewer was not insured, as he wrote to Carl that very same day: "… this loss, great as it is, I can bear." Typically for the Brewer, he was, it would seem, positively fuelled by the thought of having to build something new. "Even before the fire had been fully extinguished, this energetic man stood at his drawing board sketching, as if by the glow of the flames, a new design," wrote the sculptor Theobald Stein in his memoirs.

The Brewer himself, in a letter to Carl, declared that he was stimulated by the prospect of having to rebuild the brewery: "My strength has been fully equal to my strain, so I am perfectly fine. Working under pressure always enlivens me and increases my resilience," he wrote. "I, much like Polycrates, have known fear in my material success, and now Nemesis has appeared suddenly and unexpectedly, but I am well prepared for this and feel myself in a good state of mind about having to start more or less from scratch."

On the very same day the Brewer commissioned a carpenter to rebuild the grain store, and in the coming days he decided that subsequent structures should be in iron and not wood to reduce the fire hazard. On 1 September, the very day that the new brewing season began, the Brewer was ready to recommence brewing at the rebuilt Carlsberg. The Brewer concluded: "... the brewing then proceeded uninterrupted."

Carl received the letters from his father, with news both big and small, and felt like he was in "exile". It also certainly made him forget Emilie Djørup. In Scotland he met Ottilia Stegmann, the daughter of a Danish merchant, who would later become his wife.

That the Brewer could consider his mission accomplished can be seen from a letter written to his partner Erhard Kogsbølle around the time of Carl's homecoming.

"He has returned to me in every respect as I had hoped and anticipated. In France he has been learning to be a *chevalier*, and in England a perfect *gentleman*, in which regard he has made remarkable progress. This formal development has, nonetheless, not had the least influence on his simple bearing towards his nearest and dearest, and there is not the slightest difference to be detected between our relationship 5 years ago and now."

The rift

For all that, not everything was perfect between father and son when Carl returned home from his four years in exile in 1870. The Brewer had originally intended helping Carl to buy a brewery in a Danish country town when he came home. But in the end the Brewer decided that he would build a brewery alongside Carlsberg, an "annexe brewery", which Carl would lease and run on his own account.

In the first instance Carl brewed English ale, but the Danes were not keen on the taste, so he switched to brewing Bavarian lager beer like his father. He was full of ideas and new initiatives following his years abroad and had come to appreciate a more commercial form of production.

The Brewer, by contrast, was a child of the old guild system. For him beer was a seasonal thing. The beer should be stored ready, and the customers should wait for it. This was before the time of advertising, and that sort of thing did not interest the Brewer anyway. He had enough sales. For many years the new brewery in Valby had retained its former office in the centre of Copenhagen. When customers dropped by to order goods, they wrote their orders on a blackboard outside the door. If the board was full and the beer stocks running low, the customer was not averse to deleting a competitor's name on the board to make space for his own.

Carl wanted things to be different. He wanted to expand, export and systematise. Which is precisely what he did. And he received a good deal of help from his father. In 1873 the Brewer transferred his provincial customers to Carl, and in 1878 all the customers on the outskirts of Copenhagen. This meant that by 1879 Carl's brewery, the Annexe Brewery, was producing almost as much as the Brewer's. On more than one occasion Carl asked his father for permission to expand his brewery, which was after all rented from his father, but each time the answer was no. The Brewer did not want a brewery producing more than about forty thousand barrels annually. And Carl was already way over this limit.

In order to accommodate his son's wishes, the Brewer suggested that he should build a new brewery, and in 1879 Carl built the brewery which would later be named New Carlsberg.

Not all of Carl's enterprise was to the Brewer's liking. In particular, he was not impressed with Carl's increasing zeal for patronages, even if to a degree he had inherited it from the Brewer himself, who was one of the great benefactors of the day.

The historian Johannes Steenstrup, a friend of the Brewer, as was his father Japetus Steenstrup, wrote: "It also provoked the father's displeasure that Carl worked to such a great extent as a patron. He thereby accrued a far too easily won honour if one considers the favourable conditions under which he was able to rent his brewery and the extent to which he had been bolstered by Carlsberg's good name…"

Last, but certainly not least, the Brewer was unhappy that, in his eyes, as a result of the major expansion Carl was compromising in the one area where the Brewer could not tolerate compromise: the quality of the beer.

The disagreement between father and son on the quality of the beer was to have far-reaching consequences. On a personal level, it led to a rift which would last from 1882 to 1885, two years before the Brewer's death.

And the natural succession, which the Brewer had spent so much of his life securing through his mentoring of Carl, was broken. Carlsberg would not pass to the next generation. It would take an altogether different course.

CHAPTER 3: THE INDUSTRIAL PIONEER

In the years 1875 to 1878 a great master plan came to fruition, conceived by the Brewer, probably at his desk in the Captain's Room at Carlsberg. As always with the Brewer, nothing was left to chance. Through his investments the Brewer would cement his reputation as an industrial pioneer in Europe and one of the greatest commercial patrons Denmark has ever known. The focal point for all of this was the Carlsberg brewery in Valby, a brewery which has a special place in Danish industrial history and which has today grown into the fourth-largest brewing company in the world.

The Brewer was a leading light of the Danish brewing industry, which was one of the most expansive industries of all at the end of the nineteenth century. The number of workers in the industry increased more than fivefold between 1872 and the end of the century, and Old Carlsberg, which at that time was a Danish brewing stronghold, accounted for a good proportion.

The Brewer, however, was not a part of the new bourgeoisie, which was defined by its ownership of capital. In fact, the Brewer detested this new group.

Carl remembered a visit to Carlsberg by a stock exchange magnate, a typical "money-grabbing plebeian" who was not himself a brewer but had set up a brewery solely to make money. The man in question complained that the Brewer had reduced the price of his beer, which in his opinion was destroying the market. He recommended that the Brewer should instead put the price up and use the profits to buy bonds. The Brewer replied that it was his job to brew as well and as cheaply as possible, and that he would keep doing this even if he didn't make any money at all.

"This mindset was beyond the stockbroker, and Jacobsen had great fun at the expense of this pitiable man, who had built a brewery but preferred to invest his money in funds if they gave a better return," Carl noted.

The master plan was not a strategy which had been meticulously thought through in advance. It was more a matter of the Brewer gradually expanding his circles and unhesitatingly seizing the opportunities which presented themselves. Nevertheless, it does seem that the Brewer's investments were made with precision and considerable overview. In the course of just a few years he succeeded in establishing the Carlsberg Laboratory (1875), the Carlsberg Foundation (1876) and the Museum of National History at Frederiksborg Castle (1878).

The Carlsberg Foundation

Over a long period the Brewer had considered the idea of establishing an institution to promote science. That institution was to be the Carlsberg Foundation.

The idea had also formed in the Brewer's mind that in the

CARLSBERG IN VALBY Carlsberg still has its headquarters in Valby, where the Brewer founded the brewery. The Elephant Gate, which Carl Jacobsen had built in granite from the island of Bornholm in 1901, bears Carl's motto: *Laboremus pro patria* (Let us work for the fatherland). (Photograph of the Elephant Gate, built 1901, designed by architect Jens Vilhelm Dahlerup. Carlsberg Archive)

THE CARLSBERG FOUNDATION The Carlsberg Foundation, which shares a building on H.C. Andersens Boulevard in Copenhagen with the Royal Danish Academy of Sciences and Letters, is also crucially important today in funding research and art in Denmark.

In 2010 the Carlsberg Foundation donated around one hundred and thirty-one million kroner for Danish basic research. In the same year, the New Carlsberg Foundation, founded by Carl Jacobsen in 1902 in connection with the transfer of his New Carlsberg brewery to the Carlsberg Foundation, donated around ninety-six million kroner in support of art and the running of the Ny Carlsberg Glyptotek. (Carlsberg Foundation. Photograph: Anders Sune Berg) long term he would bequeath his entire brewery to the Carlsberg Foundation. This is evident from a letter which the Brewer sent on 17 September 1876 to the zoologist and biologist Japetus Steenstrup, who would become a member of the Carlsberg Foundation's first board of directors:

"The other day I was visited by Madvig [who would become the first chairman of the Foundation, ed.], who was very happy with the plan as he understood it. His only major objection concerned the relationship between the laboratory and the brewery, should the latter in future come into other hands, which I fully appreciated, but I informed him that this problem would disappear when, as I intended to do, I bequeathed the entire brewery to the Carlsberg Foundation."

The background to the master plan was probably multifaceted. But it is clear that the aggravated relationship between the Brewer and his son Carl played a role. The Brewer, who was now sixty-seven years old, wanted his brewery to continue as he himself saw fit. And the focal point for the continuation should be science and practical skills. As he had written to Carl previously:

"Whoever possesses the most complete understanding of chemistry and auxiliary sciences, allied with the necessary practical skill and insight, will be Europe's leading brewer in the next generation."

This needed to be secured. No longer through his son, who had disappointed him by not living up to the Brewer's quality standards in beer brewing, but through the Carlsberg Foundation, which thereby became the world's first commercial foundation. By comparison, the Carl Zeiss Foundation in Germany, one of the earliest foundations, came into being in 1889, while the Nobel Foundation in Sweden was founded in 1900.

The importance of research

In the previous year the Brewer had taken the revolutionary (by the standards of the day) step to establish a research unit, the Carlsberg Laboratory, which remains to this day an internationally acclaimed research institution under the auspices of the Carlsberg Research Centre.

Today, any self-respecting large industrial enterprise devotes extensive resources to research and innovation. But what the Brewer did, linking a research unit to an industrial company, had not been done before. On the contrary, there was widespread scepticism about mixing the two worlds. And the general view was that if educational institutions were established, it should be done through private initiative. It was not something which the public coffers should support. Here the Brewer was of a different view.

A demonstration of this came in 1855, when the Folketing (at the time the lower house of the Danish Parliament), in which the Brewer had a seat, held a debate on the establishment of the Royal Veterinary and Agricultural University. The liberal politician Anton Frederik Tscherning stated that he believed that the university should be set up on private initiative, possibly with state support, adding that the most solid basis for the development of trade was "hard work and moderation".

Tscherning was opposed by the Brewer, who declared that basic scientific education should be regarded as essential within practically all branches of trade, and that the agriculture department at the new university would have the important task of training leaders in this industry.

The Brewer was far-sighted. He saw that it was not enough for industry to demonstrate hard work and moderation. Alternative big thinking was needed if emerging industry was to succeed in the future. Education and research were very much the pivotal elements in this process, and the public coffers had to help in order for the goals to be achieved. This thinking is fully in keeping with the view which prevails today.

The Royal Veterinary and Agricultural University, which today is a faculty of the University of Copenhagen, was established with a sizeable grant.

Transparency and generosity

The Brewer never saw his brewery as a closed shop from which the outside world should be kept out. On the contrary, he kept no business secrets, and if competitors wanted his help in technical matters, he was happy to share both intellectually and materially.

When the beer at Tuborg became "sick" in 1882, the director and chairman of the board Philip Heyman turned to the Brewer, in spite of the fact that not long before he had tried to unite the Copenhagen lager beer manufacturers in opposing the Brewer for reducing beer prices. But the Brewer was not one to hold a grudge. He immediately visited Tuborg, inspected the factories and recommended various changes in the yeast cellar and some modifications in procedure. He also offered to supply Tuborg with yeast from Carlsberg.

This generosity was a trademark of the Brewer. His public spirit told him that there was more at stake than petty rivalry. For many years yeast was distributed free of charge to the locals in Valby, and right up to 1988, when the yeast cellars were closed for good, yeast could be purchased from the "yeast tower" at Carlsberg.

The Brewer's thinking is also reflected today in Carlsberg's business ethic. Here the workers are still beholden to the Brewer's "Golden Words" that the brewery should develop beer making to the greatest possible degree of perfection "regardless of immediate profit". Such a bold and binding declaration of intent might well cause a headache for any modern corporate management.

The Carlsberg Laboratory

The Brewer's spirit also continues to hover above the scientists at the Carlsberg Laboratory. An inscription on the wall of the foyer reads:

"No result of the Laboratory's activities which is of theoretical or practical importance shall be kept secret." The words are taken from the statutes of the Carlsberg Laboratory.

How different is that from the patenting practice which is universally followed within innovation and research today? The Brewer was dead by the time the first Danish patent law was enacted in 1894, and he would probably have regarded it as unnecessary.

If you were the best, there was no reason to fear competition. That is how a man who always aimed at perfection might naturally think.

Over time there has been a need to slightly alter the Brewer's words to reflect changing practice. Thus, in 1997 the statutes of the Carlsberg Laboratory were amended to read:

"The results obtained shall be published in Danish and foreign journals or in some other manner, including submission of patent applications, in order to render a public account of the activities of the Laboratory. No result of the Laboratory's activities which is of theoretical or practical importance shall be kept secret."

Knowledge and industry

The founding of the Carlsberg Laboratory had been a natural extension of the experiments which had long been part of the day-to-day life of the brewery. For many years the Brewer and his brewmasters had been conducting trials and keeping abreast of the technical literature, and the Brewer was particularly fascinated by the mysteries of fermentation. He read the French chemist Louis Pasteur's book *Études sur la bière* (*Studies on beer*), published in 1876. In the book Pasteur demonstrated that yeast was an impure product and showed a procedure for obtaining a purer yeast. Naturally, brewers throughout Europe were greatly interested.

The nineteenth century was generally characterised by a large number of scientific discoveries within physiology, bacteriology and biochemistry. These discoveries provided a breeding ground for important changes in medicine and agriculture. In Denmark, the Royal Veterinary and Agricultural University, which the Brewer had fought for in the Folketing, opened in 1858, and, as the century wore on, industrialisation really took off and several large Danish companies came into being.

On his many trips to breweries around Europe, the Brewer had seen a lot of new things which he had immediately introduced in his own brewery on returning home. First and foremost, he had learnt that the crucial starting point for successful brewing was cooling. The Bavarian beer was produced by bottom fermentation, which took place at very low temperatures. In the cellars under Valby Hill the Brewer had previously made do with cooling with natural ice and, unlike his fellow Danish brewers, avoided brewing in the summer. But in 1879 the Brewer led the way in Denmark by installing a refrigeration machine at Old Carlsberg. It was developed by Professor Carl von Linde in Munich and helped ensure the necessary cold, and hence stable beer quality.

The fact that brewing slowly became the highest energy-consumer of all industries was primarily due to these new

BEER COUNTERACTS SPIRITS Although J.C. Jacobsen was determined throughout his lifetime to run his business based on science, most people would probably feel that he got a bit carried away when extolling the virtues of beer during a lecture at the Technical Society of Denmark in Copenhagen on 16 October 1884.

This part of the lecture would also be heard as a contribution to the ongoing debate on beer taxation, which for obvious reasons the Brewer wanted to avoid, but which became a reality in 1891 after his death:

"The most gratifying thing about the greatly increased beer consumption, however, is the fact that good, cheap lager beer has proven to be one of the most powerful, and indeed most effective, means of counteracting and overcoming addiction to spirits. … It is also a fact that the Bavarian beer, even when drunk in excess, as in Bavaria, is not intoxicating because one practically never sees drunken people on the streets there and drink-related illnesses are also virtually unknown. This seems to be sufficient proof of the entirely unfounded nature of the fear which is regularly voiced that Bavarian beer will also lead to alcoholism. It seems that people forget the well-established experience from medicine that a drink which has toxic effects when consumed in concentrated form is entirely harmless, even if consumed in greater quantities, if it is drunk in a sufficiently diluted state."

One of the more curious elements in the debate of the time on beer taxation is this drawing, which was published in the satirical Christmas annual *The Octopus* in 1891 accompanied by the following text:

"You will understand how grievous a day it was for the Danish people when it became known that they had conspired to deal a fatal blow to beer, which was rightly described by the poet some years ago as one of our foremost national habits." (*The final night of tax-free beer, The Octopus*, 1891. Carlsberg Archive) refrigeration machines. But there was also a need for steam power in many other areas of the beer production. The Brewer had been one of the first to make use of the steam engine for pumping, malt crushing and hoisting. And yet more steam power was needed when it came to boiling the wort. In 1867 the Brewer switched to boiling in closed coppers under pressure using indirect steam. He had become acquainted with this system at the hands of Brewer Velten in Marseilles, but it soon became known in Denmark as the Jacobsen system and gained widespread prominence.

When new machinery was to be installed and made effective at Carlsberg, the Brewer was tireless. He could be found day and night in the cold, damp cellars under Valby Hill and elsewhere around the brewery, and he was keen to be involved in everything.

The first step in the Brewer's master plan had thus been the establishment of the Carlsberg Laboratory so that knowledge and new technology could form an ever greater basis for brewing beer. In addition to this, as we have already seen, the Brewer continually sought inspiration from abroad and purchased the latest mechanical installations for his brewery.

The breeding ground was prepared for something big at Carlsberg. And with the founding of the Carlsberg Foundation it would emerge that a sustainable structure had also been created for the brewery.

The Royal Danish Academy of Sciences and Letters

Another institution which was already well established by that time came to play an important role in the Brewer's plan when he founded the Carlsberg Foundation. The Royal Danish Academy of Sciences and Letters was founded in 1742 and had, among other things, spearheaded the first topographical survey of Denmark, thereby clarifying the map of the country. The Brewer was distinctly impressed by this assembly of learned scientists.

"The Academy of Sciences is our only institution which is so fortunate as to be independent of all outside, unscientific considerations and influences," said the Brewer.

It was therefore perhaps not all that surprising that the Academy of Sciences, headed by its president, the philologist and parliamentarian Johan Nicolai Madvig, came to play a key role in the new structure which the Brewer had conceived for his brewery.

On an autumn day in 1876 the second part of the Brewer's master plan became a reality. Having discussed the plan in detail with his lawyer, he sent a deed of gift to the Academy of

A SCIENTIST WITH A SOUL Hans Christian Oersted (1777-1851) originally trained as a pharmacist, but went on to work in a number of scientific areas. He is known first and foremost as a physicist and the discoverer of electromagnetism in 1820, but he was also a multi-disciplinary philosopher who focused on aesthetics, ethics, the holistic view and general education, holding the basic belief that everything had its starting point in the same natural laws. In 1851 he published his philosophical testament *The Soul of Nature*, which was translated into English, German and French.

Among Oersted's many initiatives was the founding of *The Monthly Journal of Literature* in 1828. The journal, which was innovative at the time, acquired almost five hundred subscribers, including the royal family, grammar schools and various reading societies, plus officials, academics and priests. Finally, there were five citizens who took out subscriptions: a plumber, a confectioner, a bell founder, a printer – and one brewer Jacobsen. This was presumably the Brewer's father, Christen, as Jacob Christian was just seventeen at that time.

Both father and son were also willing to spend money on improved learning beyond literature. The Brewer, who was a great admirer of Oersted, had paid for J.A. Jerichau's bronze statue of Oersted erected in Oersted Park in Copenhagen. When the Brewer heard that the Oxford University Museum wanted to produce a similar statue but had run into problems with a proper model, he immediately stepped in and ensured that a clay copy of the statue was purchased from Jerichau's estate and sent to Oxford. (Statue of H.C. Oersted by J.A. Jerichau, 1876. Carlsberg Foundation)

Sciences. Moreover, he sent the Carlsberg Foundation Charter, which is the primary document containing the fundamental rules governing the Foundation's functioning. He also sent the draft statutes, an appendix to the charter detailing the more specific functioning of the Carlsberg Foundation.

This just so happened to be the same day that a statue of the physicist and chemist Hans Christian Oersted was unveiled in Oersted Park in Copenhagen. The Brewer had himself helped to finance the statue of the famous scientist, who had been a member of the Academy of Sciences as well as a devotee of brewing. As previously mentioned, since his childhood the Brewer had been a great admirer of Oersted, and now through the statue he wanted to express his esteem for Oersted's illuminating enterprise.

The Brewer wrote in the deed of gift to the Academy of Sciences that he hoped that his new institute would be carried by the spirit and permeated by the light emanating from the sciences in general: "As this light has for me been a source of joy and well-being, it is upon my heart, as an instalment of my indebtedness, to also make a contribution to the promotion of sciences in general." This would now be effected through the establishment of the Carlsberg Foundation.

King Christian IX visited Carlsberg immediately after the Carlsberg Foundation had been established. The king was patron of the Academy of Sciences, as Queen Margrethe is today, and came to thank the Brewer for setting up the Foundation. The king met the Brewer's family, and the Brewer showed the king the greenhouse, the terrace, the bowery walk and Pompeii, after which the king said farewell. Afterwards, the Brewer was disappointed that the king had not expressed an interest in visiting the new laboratory.

The Carlsberg Foundation's tasks

The Brewer's intention with the Carlsberg Foundation is evident from the documents submitted to the Academy of Sciences. The Carlsberg Foundation should first and foremost continue and expand the work of the Carlsberg Laboratory. Furthermore, the Carlsberg Foundation should promote the natural sciences, mathematics and philosophy, the humanities and the social sciences through a capital of one million kroner, which would yield interest at five per cent a year after the death of the Brewer and his wife. Until then, the interest would be two per cent a year. The yield should be spent in particular on running the laboratory. The rest should be spent on promoting the above disciplines.

To this very day these tasks form the backbone of the Carlsberg Foundation's work.

The Brewer had also planned the management of the Carlsberg Foundation in detail. The Carlsberg Foundation should be governed by a board of directors comprising five members, all elected by the Academy of Sciences from among its membership. The Carlsberg Foundation's first board of directors consisted of the philologist Johan Nicolai Madvig as chairman, the historian Edvard Holm, the physiologist Peter Ludvig Panum, the zoologist Japetus Steenstrup and the chemist Christen Thomsen Barfoed. The latter two were close friends of the Brewer.

The board of directors was also to be responsible for drawing up the statutes of the Carlsberg Foundation, which could only be amended by unanimous resolution of the board. This resolution would then require the consent of the Academy of Sciences.

These provisions concerning the Carlsberg Foundation's management still apply today with just a few minor changes.

Since its inception the Carlsberg Foundation has had a major influence on Danish science and research. Right up to the period following World War II, when several private foundations and later on the public research councils appeared, the Carlsberg Foundation was the largest source of finance for Danish research.

The conflict escalates

As the conflict between the Brewer and his son escalated at the end of the 1870s, the Brewer decided to terminate Carl's tenancy of the Annexe Brewery as of 1 October 1882 in order to transfer both Carlsberg and the Annexe Brewery to the Carlsberg Foundation by bequest.

This was the final straw for Carl. He had not opposed his father's decision to establish the Carlsberg Foundation and had also sanctioned the Brewer transferring his own brewery to the Carlsberg Foundation. But Carl regarded the Annexe Brewery as his own and felt outraged.

The Brewer had also demanded that Carl refrain from using the name "Carlsberg", but on this point he did not get his way. Carl had registered his newly built brewery under the name "New Carlsberg", and this had been approved by the authorities. An agreement was subsequently reached between father and son that the Brewer would thereafter combine his two breweries under the name "Old Carlsberg" and the son could call his new brewery "New Carlsberg". Carl also received one million kroner as a paternal inheritance in return for waiving, on behalf of himself and his descendants, any further inheritance from the Brewer, and Carl duly attested his consent to his father's will, which was established on 20 February 1882. Thereafter father and son went their separate ways.

A high cost

The human costs of the split were undoubtedly considerable. Laura, who found herself in the middle of the conflict between her husband and son, paid a particularly high price. She fought behind the scenes to avert a rift, and she also fought with her own mental health. Frants Djørup, who was Carl's doctor, explained to Carl that the conflict was harming his mother's nervous system, but it was of little help.

On the inside, Laura fought to allow Carl to be able to keep the Annexe Brewery. When this proved impossible, she attended the topping-out ceremony for Carl's new brewery on 14 August 1882. The Brewer did not take part in the festivities, officially signalling the rift between father and son.

It was reported that the Brewer subsequently sealed the shutters in his dining room so that he did not have to look out at his son's new brewery. There were also several legal disputes between father and son, including over the labels on the beer bottles. And certain more visible disagreements were discussed in the newspapers of the day. Among other things, Carl had the gate between New Carlsberg and Old Carlsberg barred so that his parents could not drive along that road. Father and son also came into conflict about the name of the road running alongside the two breweries.

"Those two crazy men each put up signs down there, one bigger than the next," wrote Emil Christian Hansen, director of the Carlsberg laboratory, in his diary.

Carl was very clear in his final rejection of his father. One spring evening in 1882 he sent his staff to Carlsberg with two loads of furniture, paintings, books, and other things, gifts which he had received over the years from his father. The staff were instructed that they should unload the things in the entrance hall or, if this could not be done, then outside on the lawn and, if necessary, simply unharness the horses and leave the wagons. "My father can keep them," said Carl.

That evening, when the Brewer returned home and discovered what had happened, he went over to the Laboratory and spoke with the director.

"There was a sigh, and I felt sympathy with the old man," wrote Emil Christian Hansen.

Carl and Ottilia had eight children in all, but sadly four died very young. Their first-born, Theodora, who was born in 1877 and lived into old age, was invited some years after the rift to a children's birthday party at the home of the brewing director's daughter, Ingeborg. The family lived in the director's residence at Carlsberg. As the Brewer went past on his walk, he stopped on the road and watched the children playing in the garden. Ingeborg Schmidt recalls in her memoirs how he turned to her with a serious look and said: "Ingeborg, which of those young girls is Theodora?" He did not recognise his own grandchild.

"A black shadow lies over the twilight of my life," the Brewer wrote to Frants Djørup.

The Carlsberg Foundation's chairman, Johan Nicolai Madvig, who from the beginning had been sceptical about the transfer of the brewery to the Foundation, was concerned, as he watched the conflict between father and son escalate, about whether the Carlsberg Foundation should be involved in a dispute about the legacy. He tried to persuade the Brewer that Carl should be the legal heir to the breweries and that the Foundation should thereafter share in the profits. But the Brewer was unmoved. He wanted to lead his breweries "into the safest harbour that can be found". In his opinion, that harbour was the Carlsberg Foundation, and his will was done.

EXPERT IN BEER FERMENTATION Emil Christian Hansen, who was one of the great Danish scientists of the nineteenth century and known in the Danish press as the Nordic Pasteur, was of major importance for Carlsberg. He was the man behind the cloning of yeast cells for purified brewer's yeast, thus paving the way for later advances in microbiology.

The Brewer and Emil Christian Hansen had a sometimes strained relationship. Often the Brewer would visit the laboratory in the evening in his dressing gown and slippers to discuss the set-up of an experiment. Emil Christian Hansen wrote about one such visit in his diary: "One non-work day when I was in the process of getting an experiment up and running, he came running up to me, as he often did, with suggestions for changes. His agitation was so great that he could not wait until one experiment was finished before wanting another one to start. When he was in that mood, he worked with feverish haste, didn't pause for thought, missed out steps, mixed up one thing with another." Finally, it all became too much for Emil Christian Hansen and he stopped the Brewer with the words: "This won't do, I don't know whether I'm coming or going, now just leave it to me." The Brewer drew himself up and looked for a moment at his laboratory director. Then he shot out of the door like a rocket. (*Emil Christian Hansen in the Carlsberg Laboratory*, painting by Otto Haslund, 1897. Carlsberg Archive)

The beer smells bad

The Brewer also came under pressure in other areas in autumn 1882, when the split with Carl was final. In his will of February 1882 the Brewer had written what would later become known as his "Golden Words", which remain to this day a part of the Carlsberg Foundation Charter:

"In working the breweries it shall be a constant purpose, regardless of immediate profit, to develop the art of making beer to the highest possible degree of perfection in order that these breweries and their products may ever stand as ideal models and so, by their examples, assist in keeping the brewing of beer in this country on a high and honourable level."

But now a serious problem arose in maintaining this "high and honourable level".

The beer at Old Carlsberg had begun to acquire a bitter taste and a bad smell. Up to then the Brewer had been proud of the fact that his brewery had not changed its yeast since he had famously brought back the sample from Munich in his hatbox in 1845.

As mentioned previously, other breweries had found it easy to get access to Carlsberg's yeast if they were ever short because it was the Brewer's business ethic that even competitors should share in what was needed. But now there was apparently something seriously wrong with Carlsberg's own yeast, just as other breweries in Europe also became victims of beer sickness at the end of the 1870s and start of the 1880s.

Today we know that it was an infection with microorganisms other than the desired yeast, namely bacteria and wild yeast, which was making the beer cloudy and foul-smelling. Of course the Brewer and his scientists in the Carlsberg Laboratory did not have that knowledge. For several weeks they investigated the matter, but in vain.

It was Emil Christian Hansen, who in 1879 had become director of the physiology laboratory, who rescued the situation. His demonstration that Pasteur's purification method was incomplete and that more than one type of yeast was left in the wort after fermentation was vital in enabling Carlsberg to become the first brewery in the world to have the capability of producing a purified brewer's yeast, *Saccharomyces carlsbergensis*. This new method for cultivating brewer's yeast soon acquired a worldwide reputation.

Emil Christian Hansen's method was introduced into the brewing operations at Old Carlsberg on 12 November. In 1892, just nine years after the first brewing with the new yeast at Old Carlsberg, seven Danish and one hundred and twenty-four foreign brewers of Bavarian beer were using the new method.

This created the platform for economic and quality improvement of the beer production around the world. Now the production could be controlled, and at the same time the method was cheap to introduce.

Cultivated yeast is also used today in the pharmaceutical industry for the manufacture of drugs. Furthermore, the vast majority of wine is also today produced using cultivated yeast, which is part of the reason why poor vintages have gradually become a rarity.

Revolt against the Brewer

Nevertheless, the solving of the mystery of beer fermentation was not without its accompanying problems. Through his work Emil Christian Hansen had indirectly criticised Louis Pasteur's work. This was not to the liking of the Brewer, who was a great admirer of the French chemist, which is why it was difficult for the Brewer to acknowledge Hansen's results.

Emil Christian Hansen also made other observations. He

believed that in his old age the Brewer had ended up succumbing to the lure of absolute power.

"An administration where everyone has his area to take care of with fixed authority and corresponding responsibility is not known here. We suffer the same at the Laboratory. Here too he does as he pleases according to his mood. He can't stand it that Kjeldahl and I actually act as directors."

Johan Kjeldahl was director of the chemistry department at the Carlsberg Laboratory and world-famous for his method for determining nitrogen in compounds, known indeed as the Kjeldahl method, which he developed in 1883.

In Emil Christian Hansen's opinion, the Brewer was also stubborn when it came to using the results of his research. For example, the Brewer was opposed to implementing actual sales of yeast. The Brewer persisted in his old view that yeast should be made freely available. But Hansen noticed that other companies were now making a profit out of his discovery. At the same time, he was bitter that, in his view, he was not on a sufficiently high salary.

Things got worse in 1884 when the Brewer asked Emil Christian Hansen to write an article about his research results for an Austrian journal as on his travels the Brewer had encountered great interest in the matter. However, the Brewer withdrew the article and wrote his own version.

MICROORGANISMS AND ALPINE AIR Louis Pasteur (1822-1895), French chemist and microbiologist, and microbiology's greatest pioneer, was the guest of honour at Carlsberg in 1884, on which occasion he gave a speech for his Danish host:

"None of those here gathered will, judging by what we can see, be in any doubt that we find ourselves in a home where the demands for cleanliness are met most rigorously, yet it would be an improper disregard of the truth if I were to deny that it is the brewery's fermentation cellars, where work proceeds uninterrupted with billions of microorganisms, which in this respect really take the prize; for, whilst I with certainty may assert that masses of microbes invisibly hover about in this hall, I must nevertheless admit that in Mr Jacobsen's fermentation cellars there is an air which, in regard to purity, approaches that which is to be found at the Alpine summits." (Bust of Louis Pasteur by Paul Dubois, erected at Carlsberg. Carlsberg Archive)

LOUIS PASTEUR

This caused Hansen to respond with a letter to the Brewer:

"I am deeply saddened that you have done me this in-justice, and my sorrow is made all the greater by the fact that actual errors have crept into your rewrite. I am thinking here not of the issue of Pasteur's importance, but of what I actually stated in my work and what is not stated."

Jacobsen replied:

"I believe that regard for the Laboratory requires that all further discussion on the journal article, which is now a fait ac-compli, should herewith cease."

The Brewer regarded Carlsberg as his brewery, and he found it difficult to see that the ownership was not just about the rights to control the research results, but also to correct them.

The Brewer's public approval of Emil Christian Hansen's efforts was to come in 1884 in a lecture at the Technical Society in Copenhagen. Here the Brewer fully acknowledged Emil Christian Hansen's contribution as the saviour of Carlsberg:

"... when the yeast deteriorated, we regarded it as sheer bad luck and fell back on exchanging yeast with other brewer-ies, and this helped all the while there were still a lot of brewer-ies which did not brew in the danger season, including Carls-berg, which for 36 years had followed this procedure and had never therefore needed to change yeast. But when it became the norm to brew over the summer, the yeast became generally more and more contaminated and the endless exchanging of yeast no longer helped because there was practically nowhere that one could find a tolerably usable yeast.

"However, by the time this 'calamity', as it was justifiably called, had reached its peak, salvation was at hand because a Danish scientist at the Carlsberg Laboratory, Dr Hansen, discov-ered a highly ingenious and safe way of differentiating the in-dividual cells in the brewer's yeast from one another so that he could cultivate each individual cell by itself, following which, using a remarkable analysis method also discovered by him, he was able to determine which of the individual cells were wild and which were true brewer's yeast. Subsequently, from one of these pure cells, using the pure culture in accordance with Pasteur's excellent method, a sufficient quantity of absolutely pure brewer's yeast was developed that further development could be continued in the brewery's fermentation cellars, where propagation, which occurs roughly to the fourth and fifth powers, soon progressed so much that a large number of breweries both here in Denmark and abroad could be supplied."

Old Carlsberg the leader

Peace was finally restored a little while later when Louis Pasteur visited Copenhagen to attend the International Medical Congress. The Brewer had invited Pasteur and his wife to stay in a suite at Hotel D'Angleterre, Copenhagen's most fashionable hotel. During his stay, the French scientist also paid a visit to Old Carlsberg and the Carlsberg Laboratory, where Emil Christian Hansen met his French colleague and a dinner was held in Pasteur's honour which Emil Christian Hansen also attended. Subsequently, the Danish scientist was also invited to Paris by Pasteur.

At the same time, the Brewer was able to maintain with satisfaction that Old Carlsberg was the leader in the market.

With the establishment of the Carlsberg Laboratory the Brewer had sent out a clear signal that he viewed research and knowledge as the cornerstones of his brewery and of the new industrial society into which Denmark was developing. At the same time, with the establishment of the Carlsberg Foundation he had created the platform for enabling a proportion of the profits from the beer to benefit the whole of Danish society.

Yet the Brewer's master plan was far from finished.

CHAPTER 4: FOR FOLK AND FATHERLAND

When the Brewer was young, his father took him on an excursion into the countryside to visit Frederiksborg Castle and the royal portrait gallery. The Brewer would return regularly throughout his lifetime, and as an old man he still vividly remembered the first impression the castle had made on him all those years ago in his youth.

"It was that summer when, as a boy, I first heard the castle bells ring out over the lake in the still of the night, which captivated me instantly and filled me with a sentiment for the castle which would last my whole life."

The Brewer was an enterprising and level-headed businessman when it came to brewing. But he was also a Romantic and, like most Danes, had a special affection, bolstered by his boyhood memories, for King Christian IV's magnificent Renaissance castle, which was built around 1600 on three islands in a lake in the middle of a forested region of North Zealand.

Following the abolition of absolute monarchy in 1849, for a short period the castle once again served as the royal residence. King Frederik VII and his morganatic wife, Louise Christine Rasmussen, known as Countess Danner, spent their winters at the castle, which was built in red brick with green copper roofs, towers and spires. There was very much a fairy-tale feel about the old castle. So the whole of Denmark was hit hard when the castle burnt down on a December night in 1859.

A national cause

At that time the Brewer was forty-eight years old. Although, in the preceding years, he had given up his work in both the Rigs-dag and the Copenhagen City Council and was no longer active in politics, he had more than enough to do with his brewery, which was undergoing major development. Not to mention the fact that he was here, there and everywhere as a helper and benefactor in Copenhagen society. The mentoring of Carl was also high on his agenda in those years, albeit that summer he had sent Carl away on an educational trip with one of his teach-ers. So there was certainly nothing to suggest that the Brewer was short of work.

Nevertheless, the Brewer threw himself with all the energy he could muster into the rebuilding of Frederiksborg Castle, which quickly became a national cause. The Brewer's commit-ment to the castle was to last right up to his death, culminating in 1878 with the establishment of the Museum of National His-tory. This was the initiative of the Brewer himself, who wanted a museum to house the historical mementos of the Danish people.

The fact that just two years after the establishment of the Carlsberg Foundation he succeeded in such a complex venture, which led to the Museum of National History becoming an

FROM MANOR HOUSE TO ROYAL CASTLE The site of the castle today was occupied in the Middle Ages by the manor house of Hillerødsholm, which dated back
to 1275 and was owned by some of Denmark's noblest families. In 1560 the manor
was acquired by King Frederik II. The king was enraptured by his new property and
named it after himself: Frederiksborg. Later he began rebuilding and expanding to
turn the manor house into a fully-fledged castle. His son, Christian IV, who was born
in the castle in 1577, was responsible for the design of the castle as we know it today, which was rebuilt in his style following the fire in 1859. (K.G. Jensen's painting
of the castle, 1913. The Museum of National History. Photograph: Frederiksborg/
Lennart Larsen)

GRIPSHOLM CASTLE AS A PROTOTYPE When, shortly after the fire at Frederiksborg Castle, the Brewer visited Gripsholm Castle on Lake Mälaren in Sweden, which housed a national history museum and was built by King Gustav I of Sweden, the seed was sown that he might establish a museum at Frederiksborg Castle.

When the Brewer revisited Gripsholm Castle twenty-seven years later, in September 1886, shortly before his death, he wrote home to Laura, and from the letter it is evident that he was delighted that King Frederik VII and Countess Danner had declined to take up residence at Frederiksborg Castle after it was rebuilt, thus opening up the possibility for his dream to be realised:

"One could never have imagined that this obstacle would be so quickly removed, and no less could I have imagined that my civil enterprise would increase to such an extent that I should be in a position to become the tool for the realisation of that patriarchal idea! These thoughts intrude upon me every time I visit Gripsholm, but never as animatedly as today, when I visited this place for what will in all probability be the last time, and when a review of the last eventful period of 25 years of my life presented itself.

I must be extremely ungrateful to providence as I did not feel the need to thank God for granting me the fortune to be able to say to myself in my old age that I as a brewer, but also as a citizen, have not lived in vain and that few of my fellow citizens have enjoyed similar fortune and achieved so much for the good of the fatherland." (Gripsholm Castle, photograph, 1889. Fratelli Alinari Museum Collection, Firenze. Polfoto) independent department of the Carlsberg Foundation, demonstrates the extent of his commitment. Thereafter, the Carlsberg Foundation was financially committed to the museum, and also to ensuring its future operations, as is the case to this very day. The bringing of the Museum of National History under the umbrella of the Carlsberg Foundation cemented in place another cornerstone of the Brewer's master plan.

The money spent on rebuilding the castle was raised partly through national subscriptions and partly through contributions from the king and private individuals, including the Brewer. By contrast, the money spent on establishing the Museum of National History was solely the Brewer's. So it was not the king alone who rebuilt the old royal castle, and royals have never lived in the castle since, nor was it the nobility. As the Brewer wrote to Carl:

"We do not have much in the way of wealthy nobility, and what we do have is for the most part too poorly educated and rather too lacking in generosity to make such sacrifices for the common good. But even greater is the duty which befalls any citizen who has an abundance of income surpassing his own rather modest needs to act in this respect, and one should not be deterred from such even if for a time one must need stand alone, for by and by the power of example will take effect. At any rate, one will have the knowledge of having done one's best, and this brings far greater satisfaction than the pleasures derived for oneself alone, be they just as noble."

As the nobility no longer possessed either the abilities nor the means to be of social use, he regarded it as incumbent upon the citizenry to take the lead when it came to "sacrifices for the common good".

The Brewer became a patron who stepped in each time the work of rebuilding the castle stalled, and slowly but surely he became a particularly active benefactor, especially in regard to the museum. He took an active part in the measures that were taken from the time of the fire in 1859 and for the next twenty-eight years up to his death in 1887.

Love of the fatherland

It might at first be hard to understand why a wealthy man like the Brewer would spend almost thirty years of his life rebuilding and refurbishing an old royal castle, in which he himself would never live, and creating a museum within its walls. In those years, nouveau-riche industrialists all over Europe were building splendid palaces for their own pleasure and amusement, and the Brewer could have done likewise. But he chose to do something different.

It would be reasonable to believe that the Brewer's commitment was due to his interest in art, but this is probably only half the story. It is true that, since his youth, the Brewer had been interested in Antiquity and the classical works of the sculptor Bertel Thorvaldsen, as well as in the Italian masters and the Danish Golden Age portraits of Oersted and others he admired. But unlike his son Carl, who was passionate about art for art's sake, the Brewer identified more with art as a communicator of historical themes and messages. In the case of Frederiksborg Castle, the message was love of one's country, that is, love of Denmark.

For the Brewer Denmark was the fatherland, which he regarded it as his duty to serve. Although he had not done military service, which was introduced in Denmark following the abolition of adscription in 1788, he had been a member

THE BREWER IN THE CIVIC GUARD The Brewer was proud of his service in the Civic Guard, which he regarded as vital because this military body connected the defence of the fatherland with the citizens. (Reconstruction of J.C. Jacobsen in the uniform of the Civic Guard, watercolour, 1945. Carlsberg Archive)

of the Civic Guard, earning the title of Captain, which he used proudly throughout his lifetime:

"I want to make it clear that I am a free citizen," said the Brewer when asked by Frants Djørup to explain why he continued to use the title of Captain.

In order to understand this comment, it is important to remember the Brewer's background. His grandfather was a copyhold farmer whose farm had become freehold in 1793. Although his father had moved to Copenhagen, the Brewer's roots were firmly in the peasant, farming class, which had first formed the nucleus of Denmark's land army under the old military system, stretching right back to the Vikings, when one in ten farms had to present to the king a farmhand fit for military service. Later, in 1701, when King Frederik IV established the land militia during the Great Nordic War, one in four copyhold farms had to present a soldier, who was chosen by the landowner.

With the abolition of adscription, the farmers were no longer bonded but free citizens who slowly acquired the same rights as the country's other citizens. "Citizen", "defence" and "freedom" are thus key terms in understanding the Brewer's pride at having belonged to the Civic Guard, comprised of townsmen capable of bearing arms, which had been active since the 1500s and which undertook the important task of defending the fatherland.

The Brewer nurtured both a spirit of self-sacrifice and a feeling of duty towards the national effort, and, as he later wrote to Laura in respect of his commitment to Frederiksborg Castle, few had, like him, enjoyed "similar fortune and achieved so much for the good of the fatherland". One had to do one's bit for the fatherland whenever an opportunity presented itself. And Frederiksborg Castle was just such an opportunity.

Today, the term "fatherland" has certain undertones

with which not all Danes are comfortable. Undertones of self-sufficiency and xenophobia in a globalised world where many would rather speak of tolerance and openness. The Brewer knew a different Denmark where God, king and fatherland were national symbols, but also something substantive for which most Danes would live and die.

From united monarchy to small state

The political situation was that it was not long since Denmark had fought the First Schleswig War (1848-1850) against Germany over the duchies of Schleswig and the German-speaking Holstein and Lauenburg, all of which at that time were part of the Danish united monarchy. The war, which was one of the first nationalist conflicts of the nineteenth century, actually ended in Danish victory. However, unrest simmered in the Schleswig-Holstein regions, and the situation remained unstable.

The Brewer was sympathetic to the National Liberals, who had formulated the Eider Programme in 1842 advocating that Denmark's historical southern border at the river Eider between Schleswig and Holstein to the south should be redrawn to release Holstein and Lauenburg from the Danish monarchy while retaining Schleswig.

The situation became steadily more critical during the next twenty years or so, culminating in 1864 with Danish defeat in an unprecedentedly fierce battle. The Prussians and Austrians gave a display of the new art of industrialised warfare, incited by the Prussian Minister-President Otto von Bismarck under the now legendary slogan: "The great issues of the day are not decided through speeches and majority decisions, but through iron and blood."

Denmark was to bear the full brunt of that philosophy: three thousand Danish soldiers died, and by the time the war

CARLSBERG BEER TO THE FRONT Just one week before the key Danish defeat in the Second Schleswig War at the Battle of Dybboel, Carlsberg beer was brought to the soldiers occupying the Danish front-line positions. One soldier wrote in his diary:

"In the night [11 April 1864, ed.] a beer wagon arrived carrying warm beer. It was Carlsberg beer from Copenhagen, and it was a tasty and refreshing drink. I had my mess tin half-full of beer and had begun to drink when suddenly an incendiary bomb came straight at me. I immediately threw myself on the ground, spilling most of my beer.

"Sometime in the morning they stopped firing incendiary bombs and started up again with the shells. They were busy blowing up the bridge down to its foundations. They were using round cannonballs. We could see them land and roll along the bridge before they exploded. It wasn't long before the bridge was blown to smithereens." (*Coffee party outside the huts at the Store Dannevirke earthworks*, drawing published in *The Illustrated Times*, 7 February 1864. Carlsberg Archive) was over the Danish monarchy had lost two fifths of its territory and one third of its population. It was a terrible defeat, for which the Brewer felt a personal responsibility because as an adherent of the National Liberals he had supported the policy which had led to the disaster.

The defeat in 1864, which ended with Denmark being reduced to a small state, probably helped further strengthen the Brewer's commitment to rebuilding Frederiksborg Castle, which had burnt down five years beforehand, as a national rallying symbol at a difficult time.

Just fourteen days after the fire at Frederiksborg Castle in 1859 the Brewer had intervened. He had run a competition to submit drawings of the King's Oratory, which had been lost in the fire, and he himself donated the prize. Two other "splendour rooms" showcasing the splendour of the original seventeenth century castle were to follow, namely the Great Hall and the Knights' Room ("the Rose").

A few years later the Brewer commissioned twenty-three paintings with Biblical motifs from the promising young artist Carl Heinrich Bloch, who was one of the most expensive artists of his day. The King's Oratory, which was to house the Biblical motifs, was completed in 1871, reconstructed from old drawings and descriptions as well as the memory of artists and craftsmen. This was repeated for the Great Hall and the Rose. The artists and craftsmen carried out the work, and the Brewer paid. His objective was that everything should be reconstructed as fully accurate copies of the original rooms from the time of King Christian IV.

By 1860 the architect Ferdinand Meldahl had been appointed to undertake the rebuilding of Frederiksborg Castle. For many years to come he and the Brewer would form a strong partnership.

A national heritage

When Frederiksborg Castle had been fully recreated some years later, the question naturally arose as to what the castle should be used for. Ferdinand Meldahl and the Brewer were by now in no doubt. Frederiksborg Castle should be the venue for a national history museum.

On his many trips the Brewer had visited numerous museums. As well as Gripsholm Castle in Sweden, he was especially inspired by the Palace of Versailles in France, which he had first visited in 1855. He was impressed by how the whole of France's history was portrayed through paintings and sculptures.

The museum at Versailles had been established in 1833, when the Duke of Orleans had restored the monarchy as King Louis Philippe. Following the French Revolution (1789-1799), when the king had been guillotined, and the subsequent years of republic and empire, there was a real need to manifest national unity.

In Germany, too, where there was not yet an actual German nation, a museum had been set up to strengthen national identity. The Germanic National Museum was established in 1853 in Nuremberg to commemorate the most important events and people in the history of the Germanic fatherland.

In April 1877 the Brewer presented his plan for a national history museum at Frederiksborg Castle.

"A communing with mementos of the past evokes and forms the nation's historical sense and strengthens its awareness that it has shared in humankind's general cultural development, and thereby its recognition of the duties which this inheritance from its forbears places on those now living and on future descendants, and such awareness and recognition cannot fail to strengthen the nation's self-esteem and moral fortitude, which a small nation like ours needs to a high degree."

Such was the Brewer's reasoning for the establishment of the museum which he presented to the committee appointed by King Frederik VII shortly after the fire. In May 1877 the committee wrote to the Ministry of the Interior recommending the plan, which had been born of the Brewer's "unfailing fervour and patriotic interest for Frederiksborg", and in June of that same year the ministry responded positively.

An unrefusable gift

In January 1878 the Brewer wrote to the Carlsberg Foundation announcing that he wished to finance the interior furnishment and decoration of the King's Wing in the style of Christian IV, and that the King's Wing should thereafter be used as a venue for major ceremonial occasions in the royal family and should be home to a new national history museum.

In April 1878 King Christian IX, who had assumed the crown upon the death of Frederik VII in 1863, gave his assent to the establishment of the Museum of National History at Frederiksborg Castle. The Rigsdag did not at first like the initiative, which was the result of an individual, namely the Brewer, having a plan on which the king was now conferring the royal seal of approval, but eventually it acceded to the proposal. Ultimately, the gift was far too generous to refuse.

The museum's charter set out its objectives. The museum should: "… provide a home for inspiring, wide-ranging representations of Danish historical reminiscences from the introduction of Christianity to the present time."

The Brewer was appointed a member of the museum board, which also included the archaeologist Jens Jacob Asmussen Worsaae (chairman), the architect Ferdinand Meldahl, who was responsible for fitting out the castle as a museum and who had been appointed by the king, and the historian Edvard

Holm, who was elected by the Royal Danish Academy of Sciences and Letters. Unfortunately, it soon emerged that there were major differences of opinion between these men as to how the museum's charter should be fulfilled.

It was decided that the museum would open to the public on 17 December 1884, which was the twenty-fifth anniversary of the fire at the castle. Materials and objects had been continuously accumulated, including portraits, furniture, statues and historical paintings, and it was the Brewer's intention that everything which could not be obtained in the original should be copied.

The Brewer's plan

At the beginning of 1884 the Brewer presented a comprehensive plan for the whole museum in the form of a list of around eighty subjects for historical paintings. The idea was that the history of Denmark should be depicted throughout the castle's rooms and halls in chronological order. As the Brewer was particularly passionate about historical painting, there was a preponderance of historical paintings as well as portraits and statues.

From the Brewer's plan it can be seen that he prioritised subjects from the oldest period of Danish history, when Denmark was still a large and powerful kingdom, with the monarchs as central figures.

A year after the Brewer had presented his plan, it was mentioned for the first time in the minutes of the museum board, where Edvard Holm expressed his scepticism at the "sculptural representations of persons whose portraits are not known". He was referring to a purchase of the moment, namely an imagination-based statue of Gorm the Old, which was wanted because in 1882 a similar statue of Gorm's wife Thyra had been obtained. As Gorm and Thyra are the first historically recognised Danish royal couple, named on the two commemorative rune stones in the town of Jelling, the Brewer believed that it was inconceivable that they should not be represented in the new museum.

When Edvard Holm voted against this, the Brewer persisted: "In my opinion, it is not a matter of whether my learned friend assigns Gorm any particular historical importance, but the question must be whether the names Gorm and Thyra belong to the nation's historical archive, for which the museum is to be a home."

The Brewer had his way, but this would not be the last time that the modern critical conception of history which Edvard Holm had here introduced at Frederiksborg Castle would come to divide the waters.

Edvard Holm, a professor of history, which had been established as an independent discipline at the University of Copenhagen in 1883, believed that one must go about things scientifically and exercise historical criticism. This contrasted with the Brewer's Romantic view of the past as a type of golden age in which the national identity had been formed. From this golden age, he believed, one should reproduce the high points so as to ensure that there was an unbroken line both backwards and forwards in the national consciousness. In this context the idea of historical criticism was not a factor which could be afforded any major importance.

The Brewer's comprehensive plan involving eighty historical paintings was never realised in its entirety.

Love of the Danish folk

Right up to our time there have been art historians who have viewed the Brewer's historical paintings with scepticism, but there has always been national affection for the works of art

KING ON A CRUSADE This painting is one of the eighty paintings which were part of the Brewer's original plan for adorning Frederiksborg Castle. Danish kings through the ages were an important focal point of this plan. Christian IV was richly represented as well as a number of other kings. Here we see King Valdemar and Bishop Absalon on a crusade in 1169. (*The conquest of Arkona by King Valdemar and Bishop Absalon*, painting by Laurits Tuxen, 1894. The Museum of National History at Frederiksborg Castle. Photograph: Frederiksborg/Lennart Larsen)

KING IN PRISON King Christian II, who reigned from 1513 to 1523, was imprisoned at Sønderborg Castle for seventeen years. After 1864 he became a symbol of the lost nation. The motif of the king in prison was originally on the Brewer's list of historical motifs, but this painting was only later lodged at the Museum of National History. (*Christian II imprisoned at Sønderborg Castle*, painting by Carl Bloch, 1871. © SMK Foto. National Gallery of Denmark, Copenhagen)

THE ASSAULT ON COPENHAGEN For the Brewer, the assault on Copenhagen on 10 and 11 February 1659 was one of the most important motifs in the Museum of National History. The historical background was that for a long period Copenhagen had been under Swedish occupation. Courageously, King Frederik III helped defeat the Swedes, and the Civic Guard, of which the Brewer was a member, took part in the defence of the capital.

The Brewer, who never held back when it came to making his influence felt in what he considered to be important areas, wrote to the artist:

"It is the wish of the board that there should be a more spirited portrayal of the assailants' attack on the ramparts and that the character of the King should be more prominent among the figures portrayed in the foreground, among whom it were also desirable that one should feel more animatedly the excitement which the battle induced in them, a battle on which Denmark's future depended."

Although the assault on Copenhagen had taken place two hundred years earlier, the Brewer saw a parallel to the situation through which Denmark had just passed with the defeat in 1864. On both occasions it was the very survival of the nation which was at stake. (*The Assault on Copenhagen*, painting by C.F. Lund, 1887. The Museum of National History at Frederiksborg Castle. Photograph: Frederiksborg/ Hans Petersen) and several generations of Danes have grown up with the historical paintings as illustrations in their school textbooks.

For the Brewer there was no doubt. He was little concerned with whether the historians liked copies or reworkings of an historic event. There were more important things at stake, namely the fatherland and the self-esteem of the people themselves, the Danish "folk".

The Brewer was ready to defend the fatherland in any situation. When at the start of the 1880s he learnt that the Prussians were attempting to make German the Danish people of North Schleswig, he took up the matter and commissioned the historian Adolf Ditlev Jørgensen to write a Danish history. *Forty stories from the history of the fatherland* was duly published in 1882, and ten thousand copies were distributed free of charge in South Jutland (North Schleswig) thanks to the Brewer's financial support.

The reprinting of the book almost a hundred years later, in 1981, was a clear statement that the Brewer's historical view is still relevant. The foreword to the reprint states that, whilst the Danes' situation today cannot be compared to that of the South Jutlanders in the 1880s, the Danes must continue to maintain their cultural and historical basis and preserve their language if they are to exist as a nation in the twentieth and twenty-first centuries.

The Brewer's love of the fatherland and the Danish folk resulted in his gift to the Danish people of a Museum of National History, which today is a Danish and international attraction. Visitors get an insight into a forgotten period, and the forgotten period is made topical through various special exhibitions. Furthermore, the visitor is presented with a picture-based historical canon which existed long before such things became modern.

Another Copenhagen attraction, Christiansborg Palace,

displays Denmark's history through the woven tapestries of the artist Bjørn Nørgaard. These were a gift to Queen Margrethe on her fiftieth birthday in 1990 from a number of Danish firms and foundations as well as the French state. By contrast, the Brewer was the sole benefactor when he made his gift to the Danish people.

Many projects are launched today but often lose momentum once a few years have passed. That is not the case with the Museum of National History, and for that Denmark has the Brewer to thank. Through the ownership structure he ensured that the museum would keep running into the future. The Brewer was aware that people at that time, as well as today in a global ever-changing world, need to be told stories about who they are. He therefore spent a great deal of his personal wealth on that aim. But he was also the great patron of his time in other areas.

THE MUSEUM OF NATIONAL HISTORY TODAY The Museum of National History at Frederiksborg Castle tells the story of Denmark through portraits, historical paintings, furniture and decorative art, and it also houses a number of special exhibitions. With its beautiful landscape, Baroque gardens and the opportunity for cruises, the castle is a popular destination for excursions. The Museum of National History receives around one hundred and eighty thousand visitors every year and is an international tourist attraction. (The Museum of National History at Frederiksborg Casatle)

CHAPTER 5:
A MODERATE
MILLIONAIRE

When the Brewer set about installing electric lighting at Carlsberg in 1881, everyone was probably delighted. Light at the flick of a switch would represent a considerable step forward. However, the eagerly awaited pleasure was to be longer in coming than intended. Why? Because the Brewer was financially stretched to the limit with building and endowing the Museum of National History at Frederiksborg Castle. So he took what for him was an easy decision: he would put the project at Carlsberg on hold until his financial situation was a little less constrained. Carlsberg would have to wait for its electricity because the Brewer judged that his money was better utilised by being given away.

Very few business people today would understand this logic. Why on earth did the Brewer not prioritise essential capital spending on his brewery over what today would be regarded as excessive sponsorship activities? But the Brewer was no ordinary businessman and patron, neither by today's standards nor by those of his own time.

Although J.C. Jacobsen and his son Carl would emerge as the greatest patrons in Denmark up to World War I, the Brewer in particular did things his own way. As he put it in a letter to the actress Johanne Louise Heiberg, he was "a moderate millionaire", alluding to his motto "Work and Moderation", which he had just had inscribed in gilded letters under his name on the lighthouse at the main entrance to Carlsberg. And the Brewer's moderation benefited the whole of Denmark.

"A real shortage of funds"

The Danish word for patron is "mæcen", deriving from the Roman statesman Gaius Cilnius Maecenas, who lived shortly before the advent of the common era and of whom it was said that he had a relaxed and luxurious lifestyle, but also a great interest in art and literature. He was able to be a great benefactor within these areas because of his exceptional wealth. The Brewer was inclined neither to relaxation nor to luxury. He was wealthy, to be sure, but he also had a brewery to take care of and the coffers were not bottomless.

"Up to a few days ago, I had a real shortage of funds," the Brewer informed Johanne Louise Heiberg in 1877, when the expansion of Carlsberg was at its height and the Carlsberg Foundation had only recently been established.

Some years later, in 1883, the Brewer was again in financial straits. In a reply to a letter from Johanne Louise Heiberg requesting support for a study trip for the young tenor Lauritz Tørsleff, the Brewer confided that he had needed to take out a

LIGHT OVER CARLSBERG In 1883 a lighthouse was built at one of the main entrances to Carlsberg. It was not until 1888-89 that the Brewer could afford an electric power station to supply the whole of Carlsberg. (*Old Carlsberg's main gate from 1883 with lighthouse*, drawing published in *The Illustrated Times*, 1884. Carlsberg Archive)

amle Carlsberg.

loan to pay everybody what was owing: "You know from what I have told you that my wealth is greatly reduced, but I do not believe I said that in order to cover the extremely high costs for public spending and simultaneously for the major and essential building projects to finish Carlsberg, I have had to use my personal credit to raise a loan of eight hundred thousand kroner [corresponding to fifty-one million kroner or six million pounds in today's money, ed.], and it will be readily apparent to you that under these circumstances I need to exercise strict economy in all matters and have had to, and still now must, decline the numerous requests which I receive on a daily basis for assistance with both private and public undertakings."

Nevertheless, the Brewer still paid a sum of six thousand kroner to the young tenor "at least as an advance until such time as others may be found to contribute".

The Brewer's relationship with money was not that of a big lottery winner who carelessly splashes out on gifts until the money has all gone. Nor yet that of his fictional contemporary Ebenezer Scrooge, whose name has become synonymous with penny-pinching miserliness. The Brewer was both a successful businessman and a generous benefactor throughout his adult life.

The Brewer gave both anonymously and publicly. In the case of acts of charity, such as support for French prisoners of war following the Franco-Prussian War of 1870-71 or study trips for scientists and artists, his donations were always anonymous. His public endowments, by contrast, were obviously known to all.

The Carlsberg Foundation and the Museum of National History were far and away the two largest single initiatives of the Brewer's patronage. But they were also the culmination of many years of philanthropy towards Danish society.

THE BREWER'S PHILANTHROPY

According to Arnold Fraenkel's anniversary book on Old Carlsberg from 1897, the Brewer made donations worth 1,913,709 kroner between 1847/48 and 1886/87. According to the price calculations of Statistics Denmark, 1.9 million kroner in 1900 equates to approximately 122 million kroner in 2010. The donations were:

Donations relating to the war	27,710.31 kroner
Donations for various patriotic causes (Denmark's participation in the World Expos in Paris (1867) and Vienna (1873), the Royal Danish Theatre, the Danish Land Development Service, H.C. Oersted's statue in Oxford, N. Zahle's College of Education, contribution to the equestrian statue of Frederik VII, restoration of the Alexander frieze at Christiansborg Palace following the fire)	236,012.49 kroner
Botanical Garden's glasshouses and account thereof	26,356.72 kroner
Busts for the Royal Danish Theatre	18,587.00 kroner
H.C. Oersted's monument	19,052.63 kroner
Niels Juel's monument	23,052.00 kroner
Donations to various museums	34,995.44 kroner
Frederiksborg Castle	682,760.18 kroner
Carlsberg Foundation	845,182.63 kroner
Total	1,913,709.40 kroner

In addition, the Brewer donated 500,000 kroner for private funding, grants and "charitable causes".

Another great Danish patron of the time was Carl Frederik Tietgen. He undertook to complete Frederik's Church (the Marble Church) in Copenhagen, which had lain in ruins for many years. He succeeded, but by the time he had finished the enormous church building, he himself was close to ruin.

The Brewer did things differently. The idealistic projects in which he was constantly engaged were carried out alongside his brewing work, which financed his aspirations. And he never allowed his idealism to outstrip his finances. Perhaps that is why his patronages include many smaller projects, at least small by comparison with the Carlsberg Foundation and the Museum of National History.

Public spirit

On his trips to London the Brewer had seen the Crystal Palace, built for the Great Exhibition of 1851. All the components of the building were industrially manufactured and standardised in iron, glass and timber, and without the decoration and ornamentation which was more typical of the architecture of the day. The Brewer was greatly impressed by the structure, which unfortunately succumbed to fire in 1936. But he was just as impressed by the fact that it had been built with private funds: nine private individuals had joined forces to finance the building.

The Brewer believed that this "public spirit" was an example to follow, and he much preferred the term to "patronage". Both the design and the financing model for the Crystal Palace inspired his own greenhouse at home at Carlsberg. And the Crystal Palace was again very much on his mind in 1871 when he was given the opportunity to work on the new botanical garden in Copenhagen. As was customary when the Brewer became involved in a new project, he leapt into action, becom-

THE BOTANICAL GARDEN IN COPENHAGEN The first botanical garden at the University of Copenhagen was bestowed by Christian IV in 1600. The fourth and present university botanical garden was established in 1872-74 on a site covering roughly ten hectares close to Rosenborg Castle and the King's Gardens. The Brewer was heavily involved, both financially and practically. Today the Botanical Garden in Copenhagen is home to one of Europe's largest collections of plants, with more than thirteen thousand species from all around the world. (*The glasshouses in the Botanical Garden*, drawing published in *The Illustrated Times*, 1872. Carlsberg Archive)

ing chairman of the Business Committee, which also served as the Building Committee.

At that time the university's existing botanical garden was due to be moved to its present-day site close to Rosenborg Castle and the King's Gardens, which would entail the construction of new buildings and glasshouses. This was a job for the Brewer. He produced drawings and designs, and took the liberty of making changes to the drawings of the architect Christian Hansen, who not surprisingly withdrew from the project. The Brewer even prepared sketches for the heating systems, which he had already been responsible for at Carlsberg, and generally speaking took the building upon himself as if it were his own.

Typically, the Brewer found it difficult recognising obstacles when he first started a project. In April 1872, when the masons in Copenhagen went on strike, the masons working on the botanical garden were not initially involved. But when the strikers expressed their dissatisfaction that work was continuing at the botanical garden, the Brewer felt compelled to write to Copenhagen's commissioner of police, indirectly threatening to take the law into his own hands if peace were not maintained at the botanical garden, which fortunately it was.

When the work on the new botanical garden in Copenhagen was completed in the summer of 1874, the University of Copenhagen had a new venue for its botanical research and Copenhageners had a beautiful public park for their recreation. In connection with the university's quadricentenary in 1879, the Brewer joined with the gardener Tyge Rothe to write a paper on the garden's glasshouses, partly as a thank you for the honorary doctorate which the university had conferred on him for his work in this regard. The paper was entitled *A description of the glasshouses in the university's botanical garden in Copenhagen, with details of the garden's grounds and their arrangement 1871-1874.*

The Brewer also contributed financially to the building of the glasshouses.

Busts for the theatre

Another example of a lavish benefaction was a series of marble busts for the Royal Danish Theatre. When the original "King's Theatre" dating from 1748 became too small, a new theatre was built alongside the old one. The Royal Danish Theatre, which opened in 1874, obviously needed ornamentation, and here the Brewer, who was a regular theatre-goer, saw an opportunity to help.

The Brewer offered to ornament the theatre with marble busts of the playwrights Ludvig Holberg, Johannes Ewald, Johan Herman Wessel, Adam Oehlenschläger, Johan Ludvig Heiberg, Carsten Hauch and Henrik Hertz, the actors Johan Christian Ryge, Ferdinand Lindgreen and Anna Nielsen, and the composers Christoph Ernst Friedrich Weyse and Friedrich Kuhlau.

The series of twelve marble busts was to be produced by the sculptors Herman Vilhelm Bissen and Theobald Stein. The only condition attached to the undertaking was that the foyer, where the Brewer wanted the marble busts to be erected, should be decorated in a suitable fashion. Unfortunately, the theatre manager and the Minister for Ecclesiastical Affairs and Public Instruction were not happy with this condition. They believed that the marble busts were better suited to display elsewhere in the theatre as it was intended using the foyer as a venue for refreshments.

At first the Brewer responded with a tactical countermove. He expanded his offer to include a sum of twenty thousand kroner for the foyer's other decorations. This was a tactic he had used before in similar situations. But the theatre management and the minister stood their ground. The Brewer's offer was rejected and he withdrew it. He did not want to see the foyer, which he regarded as the theatre's assembly hall, deployed as "a public house with foaming tankards of beer and clanking soda bottles".

The marble busts – actually thirteen in all after the Brewer commissioned an additional bust of the actress Johanne Louise Heiberg – were instead erected at Carlsberg, where they stood for several years. In 1882, when the Royal Danish Theatre acquired a new manager, the Brewer succeeded in getting his marble busts into the foyer, where some of them can still be seen.

The Danish diva

It was not by chance that a bust of Johanne Louise Heiberg had been added to the series intended for the Royal Danish theatre. The Brewer had met the Danish actress in 1868 when they were both in their late fifties. They developed a close friendship and regular correspondence. In addition to getting on well, they shared the desire to help artists in various ways.

Like all other Copenhageners of the time, the Brewer was familiar with Johanne Louise Heiberg and had often seen her on stage at the Danish Royal Theatre, where she was a fêted actress. Furthermore, the Brewer and she most likely moved in the same social circles. When the Brewer first approached her, however, she had given up acting herself and was involved in helping young actors. The two of them struck up an unofficial partnership, with the Brewer donating anonymously and Johanne Louise Heiberg providing help to actors who needed it.

One of those in need was the opera singer Doris Pfeil, who was helped to study in Paris. Subsequently, the Brewer recommended continuing to help young talented performers.

THE GREAT LADY OF THE THEATRE Johanne Louise Heiberg (1812-1890), who came from a poor family, was taken on as an eight-year-old girl by the Royal Danish Theatre's ballet school and became the leading Danish actress of the Romantic era. Almost all the Danish playwrights of the age, from Adam Oehlenschläger to Henrik Hertz, wrote parts for her.

Her acting combined melancholy, coquetry and eroticism with grace and romantic charm. She was married to the author and theatre manager Johan Ludvig Heiberg. After his death in 1860, she worked as a stage director.

Her life has fascinated posterity, partly due to her memoirs, *A life relived in memory*, from 1891-1892. (N.W. Marstrand's portrait of Johanne Louise Heiberg/Pätges 1858/59. The Museum of National History at Frederiksborg Castle. Photograph: Frederiksborg/Hans Petersen)

"It has been a source of great satisfaction for me to be able to grant you a small token of my appreciation through the support which I have given your protégée, Miss Pfeil, and the most gratifying fruits which your influence on her development has borne encourage me, now that she no longer needs my assistance, to offer a similar contribution for the benefit of the artistic development of the emerging talents of your choosing. I know there are many such talents, but you yourself will best know whom might most benefit from a little support, and I therefore wish this year to make available to you a sum of five hundred rix-dollars for the stated purpose, asking you to use this money as you see fit without mentioning my name."

The anonymity was essential for the Brewer. By and by, however, the identity of the generous donor became common knowledge.

Under examination

The relationship between the Brewer and Johanne Louise Heiberg was not unlike that which she enjoyed with many powerful men of the time. She loved inviting men for dinners-for-two at her home, where, ever the charming lady, she was undoubtedly fine company. Shortly after the Brewer and she had instigated their partnership to help actors, Johanne Louise Heiberg duly invited the Brewer for dinner.

The Brewer later described the visit in a letter to Carl:

"I had not dreamt that I should ever enjoy the enviable honour, desired in vain by so many, of being invited by Madam Heiberg to a private dinner and spending four hours alone with her. I am not so foolish as to imagine that my company and my entertainment were of any particular pleasure for her, and I know full well that she wished to demonstrate her appreciation for my assistance in Miss Pfeil's training and perhaps lay claim to assistance at some future time, but I still feel with some just-ification flattered that she gave me her appreciation in this way. In any case, it helps me to confirm the level of education which I have attained in other people's eyes, and I cannot but be de-lighted that my largely self-taught endeavours have secured me such a grade from such an examiner."

It is probable that Johanne Louise Heiberg did indeed want to "lay claim to assistance at some future time". And in-deed the assistance was considerable in the coming years, when the Brewer financed a foreign trip to Switzerland and Italy for her and her two daughters after she had fallen ill. Furthermore, the Brewer assisted in obtaining Johanne Louise Heiberg a new place to live in Copenhagen and helped her with the rent, as well as giving her many gifts right up to his death.

The Brewer's office bore visual testimony to the special place which Johanne Louise Heiberg held in his heart. On his desk stood two framed photographs. On the right, his wife Laura; on the left, his friend Johanne.

For her part, Johanne Louise Heiberg did not show much sororal solidarity with the wives of the men with whom she as-sociated, referring to them as "the madams". Laura, for her part, was clearly jealous. Yet in keeping with the gender role pattern of the day she probably went to great lengths to keep a tight rein on this emotion and respect her place.

The photograph which ended up on the Brewer's desk was originally a present to Laura, for which Laura thanked Johanne Louise Heiberg in a letter:

"You have shown us lesser women such infinite beauty and nobleness, both on and off the stage, that we must beseech God to grant you many happy years in which to be active."

Johanne Louise Heiberg probably came near to the female ideal of which the Brewer once told Carl he dreamt: "a noble woman of such esteem that one might approach with humility." In any case, Johanne Louise Heiberg was probably the only person whom the Brewer ever allowed to be his "examiner".

The school builder

The Brewer was a generous giver in many other areas too. For many years he was involved in building a school in Copenhagen for Natalie Zahle, who was a pioneering educator and a fervent believer in women's right to education.

The Brewer's friendship with Natalie Zahle led to him helping her both financially and practically in this building process, among other things by designing the central heating system.

According to Birgitte Possing's biography of Natalie Zahle, the Brewer donated a total of forty thousand kroner to build the school, and he also loaned her twenty-seven thousand kroner, which made him by far the most generous contributor. On the day in 1876 when the foundation stone of the school building was laid, Natalie Zahle wrote to the Brewer, "to whom I am considerably indebted that everything has been able to start up".

She also asked him for help in the building phase. Could he come and see whether everything was proceeding correctly? Was it her or the contractor who was responsible for the topping-out ceremony? Nathalie Zahle sought answers to these sorts of questions from the Brewer. When shortly before

FEMALE SCHOOL PIONEER Natalie Zahle (1827-1913) was a headmistress and a leading figure within women's education in Denmark. Furthermore, like the Brewer she was patriotic and sympathised with the National Liberals.

She set up a private educational establishment for girls and women in Copenhagen in 1851, and the following year took over a private girls school and laid the groundwork for a school complex for women focused on training for female teachers. In 1877 she built her own school, with financial and practical assistance from the Brewer, which is still in operation today. (Carlsberg Archive)

the topping-out ceremony in 1877 a bricklayer fell from some scaffolding and died, it was the Brewer to whom Natalie Zahle turned. The Brewer also acted as one of the school's two arbitrators for a number of years.

When the Brewer died in 1887, the annual school prospectus was in the middle of being printed. Natalie Zahle put the printing on hold so that she could include her obituary of the Brewer, in which she wrote:

"We could not end without expressing gratitude to this rare friend of the fatherland for all that he has been and for this school (…) the whole life within the school's walls, its spirit and its work were in his thoughts and his heart, so in him we are truly losing a genuine and loyal friend."

Johanne Louise Heiberg and Natalie Zahle, so prominent in their own different roles, each joined forces with the Brewer in a shared mission: in Johanne Louise Heiberg's case the distribution of money to needy artists, and in Natalie Zahle's case the setting up of a school institution. But the Brewer's friendship with the two women also indicates that he was comfortable in the company of strong, female personalities. Both women, as different as they were in mind and appearance, were gifted and possessed an exceptional strength of will, as well as being enterprising like the Brewer himself. They fully lived up to his ideal of self-activity.

It was not only self-active women, however, who benefited from the Brewer's generosity. He was also a discreet giver when his other friends were in need.

In 1850 Frants Djørup was travelling in Italy when he received a letter from the Brewer containing "travel aid".

"I should be delighted, dear Frants, if in this way I might contribute in some small way to you deriving the greatest benefit from your trip."

A most splendid gift

The gift from the Brewer which would represent the biggest endowment to Danish society was the Carlsberg Foundation. When the Carlsberg Foundation was founded, Johanne Louise Heiberg wrote to the Brewer:

"Everyone in the city is talking about your splendid gift to the fatherland, and I hope that others are no less admiring of you for it than I because in truth you deserve the gratitude of us all, great and small. I hope this regal gift will bear fruit for your fatherland."

On the same day she wrote to another friend, clarifying what she meant about the Brewer's gift being discussed in the city.

"It vexes me to hear people saying that Jacobsen's splendid gift is all vanity. They derive no other pleasure in it, the miserable wretches."

Then, as now, some people had a problem with too much generosity: the giver simply must have a hidden agenda.

It is not seemly to question motives when it comes to the giving of gifts. However, it may help to balance the picture of the Brewer if we dare to pursue the line of inquiry a little. It is not inconceivable that vanity may have been a part of the explanation for his extensive patronage work over the years. The Brewer may subconsciously have been determined to win the social equality with his associates which was not his by birth. This is hinted at in several contexts, including the relationship with Johanne Louise Heiberg, whom after their first meeting he likened to an examiner who had assessed the level of education which he had attained thanks to his "largely self-taught endeavours".

Generally speaking, there was a conflict in the Brewer's character, including in regard to his patronages. He may have referred to himself as a "moderate millionaire", and the truth is that in many personal situations he was indeed moderate, but when there were guests at Carlsberg, it was as if the Brewer shed his moderate skin.

A nine-course dinner

Nanna, who served in the house at Carlsberg for a number of years, tells us that for dinner parties they served nine courses and as many different types of wine. Carl noted in this regard that even the Roman caesars had never served more than four types of wine during a meal.

The Brewer insisted that he wanted to bring people together. One might object that it could have been done with slightly less excessive fare.

Deep down, the Brewer probably wanted to impress a little.

"My house and my soirée made a fine impression on every-one, most naturally on the outsiders," the Brewer said after one gathering.

At the same time, the Brewer was aware that his deal-ings with others were somewhat affected. In a letter to Carl he expressed the feeling of inferiority which he had experienced throughout his lifetime in relation to other people. He repeat-ed his awareness that others had enjoyed a different level of education to himself, although as a middle-aged man he felt he had come to terms with his feeling of inferiority:

"It took a long time for me to overcome my dislike and fear of 'outside' associates or acquaintances who in many respects were at a different level of education to me, but it is with them that I have achieved my greatest growth, without them I would have become what I was well on the way towards – narrow-minded, dry, heavy, boring and old before my time."

Nevertheless, any inferiority which the Brewer may have

had, and for which, in any case, he partly compensated by demonstrating an uncharacteristically conspicuous extravagance when inviting people to parties at Carlsberg and by being more than ordinarily generous in many situations, is only a small piece of the explanation for his extensive patronages.

Other viable explanations have already been touched upon.

When Carlsberg burnt down in 1867, the Brewer wrote to Carl: "I, much like Polycrates, have known fear in my material success, and now Nemesis has appeared suddenly and unexpectedly."

The Brewer's fascination with the philosophies of Antiquity led him to think of the Greek goddess Nemesis, who prosecutes excess with unswerving vengeance. But very few people will believe that this should have caused the Brewer, as a sort of propitiatory sacrifice, to begin giving away large amounts of money for the benefit of society.

From beginning to end the Brewer helped his country and his people, fatherland and folk, through lavish donations because he believed it was his duty as a brewer and as a citizen. Civic duty was deeply ingrained in him and resulted not least in him also being politically active for almost his entire adult life.

CHAPTER 6: CIVIC DUTY CALLS

The Brewer was a young man of thirty-one when he entered politics as a member of the Copenhagen City Council in 1843. This was to be the start of many years of political service, partly at local level in the Danish capital, and partly at national level when later he served two terms as a member of the Rigsdag.

The Brewer never reached the front benches as a politician. In the Copenhagen City Council he was first and foremost a practical politician who was an energetic member of various committees dealing with all manner of issues from the capital's water and gas supply to steamship berths in the Port of Copenhagen. He had not yet entered the national political arena when Denmark acquired its constitution in 1849, but later he campaigned loyally for both the constitution and the universal franchise during some difficult years for Denmark.

At the time when the Brewer was first elected onto the Copenhagen City Council, he already had plenty to do getting the new Carlsberg brewery in Valby up and running, and he had also become a father to Carl just a year before.

There are no statements from the Brewer himself on why he went into politics. However, just as the explanation for a large part of the Brewer's patronage work is to be found in his perception of himself as a citizen, our understanding of J.C. Jacobsen the politician also starts there.

The Brewer's comment to Frants Djørup that he considered himself a free citizen was more than just rhetoric. For him, being a free citizen really did carry certain duties. He saw the defence of the fatherland as a civic imperative, as attested when he joined Copenhagen's Civic Guard as a nineteen-year-old, and presumably he also viewed his work in the Copenhagen City Council in the same light.

National defence and politics

The history of the Copenhagen City Council touches upon both national defence and politics.

When the Swedes stormed Copenhagen on 11 February 1659, the attack was repelled. This was due in particular to the efforts of the ten thousand Danish and Dutch soldiers who took part in the defence of the capital, but it was Copenhagen's citizens who were heralded as the capital's saviours.

King Frederik III rewarded Copenhagen's citizens by giving them a share in privileges which up until then only the nobility had enjoyed. The most important privilege was the right to elect thirty-two representatives from among the city's prosperous merchants and craftsmen to govern the city's affairs. This would be done, however, in conjunction with the Corporation of Copenhagen, comprising three to four burgomasters and six to eight aldermen, which represented the Crown.

Although the Corporation still therefore had the final say

and the city's self-government was consequently rather limited, all in all it was a step in the right direction for the citizens to have a place at the political table.

In 1840 an attempt was made to achieve a more reasonable balance of power between the two institutions with the introduction of a new municipal reform. This created the basis for modern municipal government. The assembly of thirty-two citizens, which as time went by had become self-elective, was replaced by a people-elected City Council of thirty-six members.

Nevertheless, municipal self-government in Copenhagen continued to be dominated by bureaucracy, and the officials still regarded themselves as somewhat superior to the citizens whom they had been put in place to serve. Furthermore, the right to vote and eligibility for election were conditional upon citizenship, payment of tax and possession of property, as a result of which just 1.6 per cent of the inhabitants of Copenhagen were entitled to vote in the first elections in 1840.

"Capable, libertarian and independent"

It was on this version of the Copenhagen City Council that the Brewer would serve from 1843 to 1857.

The leading newspaper of the National Liberals, *The Fatherland*, had recommended that its readers vote for J.C. Jacobsen, calling him "a capable, libertarian and independent man". The Brewer was duly elected onto the Council, which included Orla Lehmann and Ditlev Gothard Monrad, both of whom would later become ministers.

The Brewer also became acquainted with Lauritz Nicolai Hvidt, the chairman of the Council. This meeting proved to be important for the Brewer as he deemed the Danish businessman and politician, who was thirty years older than himself, to be a fine role model.

A DANISH STATESMAN L.N. Hvidt (1777-1856) was a theology graduate, but later he took over his father's commercial business. He became one of the country's leading shipowners and from 1835 to his death was director of Danmarks National-bank (the Danish central bank).

He had been a member of the Assembly of the Estates of the Realm in Roskilde from 1835 to 1842. The Brewer also sat in the assembly for a short period until the adoption of the constitution in 1849 led to the abolition of the assemblies in Roskilde and Viborg.

As chairman of the Copenhagen City Council, L.N. Hvidt led the popular march to Christiansborg in March 1848, which resulted in the setting up of the Moltke government, in which he became a minister. He helped to draft the June constitution of 1849, but retired from government in protest at the partition of Schleswig.

L.N. Hvidt was one of the Brewer's "household gods", together with the sculptor Bertel Thorvaldsen and the physicist H.C. Oersted. This bust of N.L. Hvidt was later displayed at Carlsberg alongside busts of Thorvaldsen and Oersted. (Bust of L.N. Hvidt by Vilhelm Bissen, 1877. Carlsberg Archive)

Lauritz Nicolai Hvidt was one of the older generation of National Liberals, with whom the Brewer sympathised. They were a political grouping which, though not an organised party as such, exerted a significant influence on developments in Denmark from 1840 to 1870, not least through their opposition to absolute monarchy and their support for the constitution.

The National Liberals consisted mainly of academically educated officials and were quickly dubbed the "Professor Party". From the 1830s onwards they built up an extensive network, in particular through *The Fatherland* and personal contacts.

The National Liberals were inspired by classic English liberalism, and they assigned the state an important role in social development. They believed that they represented unity vis-à-vis other social groups, and that the middle class was entitled to govern the people. Orla Lehmann, who belonged to the younger generation of National Liberals, believed that "the gifted, the educated and the rich" should have a deciding influence in the Landsting (at the time the upper house of the Danish Parliament) to protect against "the evil instincts of the plebeian mind".

The Brewer was in full support of this limited franchise and shared the fear of "mob rule", to which he referred on several occasions. Here at the end of the nineteenth century there was still fear of the revolutionary ideas which had sprouted in Europe in the wake of the French revolution at the end of the eighteenth century and the uprisings around Europe in 1848, which became known as the Year of Revolution.

The Brewer set great store by the fact that he was an independent citizen who did not belong to a particular party. Yet there is no doubt that his political affinities lay with the National Liberals.

As a Copenhagen councillor from 1843 to 1857, the

Brewer was a member of the Port Administration and of the Poor Relief System Management, and he was active in a whole range of other areas: the city's cleanliness; duties and taxes; the setting up of public bath and wash houses and butcher's stalls; grain, coal and salt measuring; and much more.

In political life the Brewer had the opportunity to bring his influence to bear and to help in a very practical way, which appealed to him greatly.

A fire trap

Consequently, it annoyed the Brewer when political bureaucracy prevented a matter being dealt with quickly and effectively. This was illustrated in 1851 when he became a member of a Royal Commission tasked with modernising the Copenhagen Fire Brigade. At that time Copenhagen was a fire trap. The density of the people and buildings, allied with the use of open fires and the prevalence of timber houses, constituted a very real fire hazard within the ramparts.

In 1863, when still nothing had been done because the plans had been shelved in the Rigsdag, the Brewer, who by that time was also a member of the Rigsdag, attempted to get things moving again by questioning the Minister for Justice. He wanted a complete overhaul of Copenhagen's fire regulations, which dated back to 1805, and simplification of the fire brigade set-up, which was overly hierarchical and unwieldy in practice.

The Brewer had already known several fires in his lifetime. Frederiksborg Castle had burnt down in 1859, and in the following year another blaze caused extensive damage in the centre of Valby. Some of the families afflicted by that fire had found shelter at Carlsberg. Later the Brewer was to experience first-hand the blaze at Carlsberg itself. In 1883 he attempted to improve the situation on his own initiative by donating a steam fire engine to the Copenhagen Fire Brigade, and at his own expense he sent an engineer to Germany to seek inspiration for improving Copenhagen's fire preparedness.

Tepid eel soup

In other areas, too, Copenhagen was very tardy in making meaningful investments for the common good. As far back as early 1853 the Copenhagen City Council had resolved that the capital should have a new water, gas and sewerage system, but no agreement could be reached on the practical implementation. Later that summer this was to prove fatal when a cholera epidemic broke out in Copenhagen.

Cholera is a contagious gastrointestinal disease caused by infection with a waterborne bacterium. The patient is at risk of dying within a few days from diarrhoea and consequent fluid loss. In Copenhagen, the doctors had more or less been expecting an epidemic because the drinking water situation in the capital was so catastrophically bad.

"Tepid eel soup" is how Copenhageners described their drinking water, which they mainly obtained from three lakes – Peblinge Lake, Sortedams Lake and Sankt Jørgens Lake – established as reservoirs for the citizens of Copenhagen. A small proportion of the drinking water also came from Emdrup Lake north of Copenhagen.

The water from the lakes flowed through hollowed-out logs into the city's pumps. It was neither purified nor filtered, and often contained bits of vegetation and small animals. Sometimes an eel became stuck in the pump's mechanism and the pump had to be dismantled to remove the eel before it began rotting.

The sanitary conditions in the capital were similarly awful. There were no toilets. Instead, people would use a small shed in the yard built over a brickwork tank which slowly filled up. Once or twice a year the "nightman" came to empty the contents of the tank into his "chocolate wagon". When the wagon was full, it was driven out to the latrine pits on the edge of the city and unloaded. If the nightman did not come, the tank would overflow. Similarly, as the nightman's wagon was not sealed, rubbish and excrement often spilled onto the streets, where there were no drains to aid their removal.

By the time the cholera epidemic had subsided at the end of autumn 1853, almost five thousand Copenhageners had died out of a population of approximately one hundred and forty thousand.

It was clear to everyone that something needed to be done urgently. In 1854 the Brewer joined a committee supervising the work of building a gasworks and a waterworks in Copenhagen. Loans were taken out, and in 1855, while he was in London, the Brewer made contact with the English civil engineer James Simpson. Through Simpson the building work was assigned to the English contractor Cochrane & Co.

When the work was ready to start in 1857, the Brewer was asked to lay the foundation stone. It was not then long before Copenhagen homes were enjoying clean water, in no small measure due to the efforts of the Brewer.

A difficult period

When the Brewer stood for the Folketing in 1854, it was in protest.

Denmark had been through a difficult period, which had ended with peaceful revolution, the abolition of absolute monarchy after one hundred and eighty-eight years, and a new constitution.

The National Liberals were a key element in these changes.

They were part of the revolutionary wave which rolled through Europe in those years, taking a different course in each country, but always rooted in the Enlightenment and the ideas of the French Revolution on liberty, equality and fraternity which had led, among others, to the July Revolution in France in 1830.

In Denmark, the peaceful revolution was driven primarily by the National Liberals. Another significant player was the Society of the Friends of Peasants, which represented the peasantry. Why should the nobility retain its privileges, people were asking. Reform and change were needed.

But although Denmark had acquired a new constitution, which entered into force on 5 June 1849, the problems in the south of the Danish united monarchy still festered.

With the First Schleswig War of 1848-1850 Denmark had, in fact, created peace in Schleswig-Holstein, at least on the surface of it. But this was by no means a final victory because the nationalist conflict remained unresolved. The pro-Germans were demanding independence from Denmark and the assimilation of Schleswig into the German Confederation. The pro-Danes, on the other hand, wanted a Denmark as far as the River Eider. The conflict was further fuelled by a rather heavy-handed language policy on the part of the Danes, including the introduction of a Danish educational and ecclesiastical language in parts of Schleswig.

The Great Powers which had brokered the peace accord in 1850 wanted the Danish united monarchy to be maintained in order to ensure European peace. The talk was of the European necessity. At the same time, they wanted to contain the unrest in the duchies and believed that Denmark had to make concessions in this matter.

In order to accommodate the Great Powers, successive Danish governments agreed to compromises. The "June constitution" of 1852 was limited to only applying north of the river Kongeåen, while the "joint constitution" of autumn 1855 was only a half-hearted attempt to retain the united monarchy.

The Brewer was against this undermining of the constitution.

Breach of constitution

Especially following the adoption of the joint constitution, the Brewer was in agreement with a large proportion of the Folketing, which talked of coup d'état and breach of constitution. The Brewer allied himself with the protest movement, urging the Danish people to join the newly established Constitution Defence League.

The Brewer wasted no time in acting upon his convictions. In the election of 2 August 1854 he stood for the Folketing and was duly elected. His message was a defence of the constitution, but it was to be several years before the country's constitutional position was resolved.

The Brewer left the Folketing in 1857, but in 1861 he decided to stand again. This time it was the issue of Schleswig which brought him to national government. He sat for two years in the Folketing, after which he became a Crown-nominated member of the Landsting, where he served until 1871.

It was in these years at the start of the 1860s that the Brewer really got close to the events which would culminate in war.

On 29 October 1863 the Brewer hosted a dinner at Carlsberg for his colleagues in the Council of the Realm, which had been revived a decade before to deal with legislative issues relating to Denmark and Schleswig-Holstein and Lauenburg. The government had put forward a proposal for a new constitution which would cover Denmark and the duchy of Schleswig, tying Schleswig more closely to Denmark. This proposal was dynamite given the tense situation in the south.

Nevertheless, the champagne corks popped at Carlsberg and the Brewer raised a special toast to both the king and the people of Schleswig. A few weeks later, on 13 November 1863, there was great jubilation among the supporters of the constitution when the "November constitution" was adopted in the Council of the Realm. There was a stubborn resolve that Denmark should remain large and powerful.

Hurrah for the king!

Prussia, led by Otto von Bismarck, was not slow in demanding a repeal of the November constitution. When the Danish government refused, Prussia announced its intention, together with its ally Austria, to occupy Schleswig. This was on 31 January 1864, and the words were soon backed up with action. War quickly became a reality.

On 5 February the Danish army abandoned the Dannevirke defensive earthworks without a fight and retreated to Dybboel. The announcement of this sent Copenhagen into uproar, and there were widespread demonstrations in the streets. The Danish commander-in-chief, General de Meza, was duly relieved of his command.

On the night when the Danish soldiers left the Dannevirke, the temperature had plummeted to minus ten degrees and there was a biting wind. Ten men froze to death, one hundred and twenty were captured, and one hundred and seventy-three deserted. This was followed by two months of heavy bombardment, and on 18 April the Prussians took Dybboel. The Minister for Defence ordered that Fredericia – which was the last bastion in Jutland – should be abandoned, after which the Prussians and Austrians occupied Jutland up to Limfjorden.

Sea battles followed, including the Battle of Helgoland on 9 May 1864. A ceasefire was declared, and the British Secretary of State for Foreign Affairs, Lord John Russell, led the negotiations between the parties, which centred on the partition of Schleswig. The negotiations subsequently collapsed.

Although the Danish armoured warship Rolf Krake tried to thwart them, on the night of 29 June the Prussians succeeded in taking the island of Als. On 3 July the Danish and Prussian soldiers clashed in the village of Lundby south of Aalborg in northern Jutland. That night, ninety-eight Danish soldiers died, while only three Prussian soldiers lost their lives. This triggered a series of Danish defeats, and for a time Denmark's very existence was under threat.

From the young girl Nanna we know a little about the Brewer's attitude to the war. He turned his anger on the media, which he believed were not promoting the cause of the fatherland. At the same time, he persistently championed the king as a unifying figure in a difficult period. Following an evening party, the Brewer returned home hoarse from shouting hurrahs to the king.

Furthermore, the Brewer did as he always did when difficult situations arose. He took action. In this situation by offering financial aid to the families of fallen soldiers, even though he was not able to keep up with the need.

"All sorts of people make private requests which Uncle cannot meet. His name has become known for his gifts to the army," Nanna wrote.

But the aid and good will were to no avail. The battle was lost, and an armistice was concluded on 20 July. At the subsequent peace conference in Vienna on 30 October 1864, Denmark was forced to relinquish Schleswig, Holstein and Lauenburg. Denmark was thereby reduced to a small state, and it has been asserted in many quarters that it is this defeat which has determined the Danish self-understanding right up to the present day.

The Brewer as a defence politician

We can only guess the Brewer's thoughts about himself and his country in relation to the defeat. What we do know is that in the years following the defeat he was heavily involved in the defence of the fatherland, which had now been significantly reduced in both area and population.

The Brewer became chairman of the Defence Commission, which was set up by the government in 1866 and gave its assessment in the same year.

The Defence Commission concluded – not surprisingly – that it saw the North German Confederation as Denmark's chief enemy. The North German Confederation, which existed from 1866 to 1871, consisted of twenty-two independent states in Northern Germany under Prussian control, with Chancellor Otto von Bismarck at the head, and represented the transition from the German Confederation to the founding of the German Empire. It also concluded that Denmark had to try to acquire allies by amending its foreign policy, and that Denmark should be divided into two defence zones: one covering Funen and Zealand, and the other covering Jutland. This division exists to this very day.

In November 1866 the Brewer hosted a party at Carlsberg. The guests were members of the Defence Commission and of the Rigsdag. The Brewer's first toast was to the new army and navy plan, of which he referred to himself as the godfather. He ended by toasting the Peace of Prague, which had been signed in August of that year after the Prussian-Austrian War, which Prussia had won.

After the war in 1864, when Prussia and Austria had been united against Denmark, Austria had gained joint ownership with Prussia of the conquered duchies of Schleswig and Holstein. Austria now relinquished this joint ownership with the Peace of Prague. At the same time, under French pressure a paragraph 5 was added to the agreement which opened up the possibility of the northern districts of Schleswig being ceded to Denmark once the population had approved this in a free vote.

This paragraph 5 had given the south Jutlanders fresh hope of being reunited with Denmark. As we know, however, this was not to happen until much later. Paragraph 5 was actually repealed in 1878, which sent shock waves through South Jutland and the rest of Denmark. It was only in 1920 that North Schleswig, the present-day South Jutland, "came home to Denmark" and King Christian X was able to ride over the border on his white horse. This event subsequently became a symbol that not all was lost for little Denmark.

The Brewer could not predict this historical development when he stood up with his wine glass at Carlsberg on a November evening in 1866 and toasted the Peace of Prague. But he fastened upon the fact that there was now hope: an opportunity had been created for the pro-Danes to return home.

A safeguard for the whole nation

The Brewer spent much of his life and wealth making the Danes proud to be Danish again after 1864. It is difficult to know how much the Brewer regretted his political contribution to the war. To what extent did he see his patronage of Frederiksborg Castle as a type of atonement? And to what extent did he simply want to strengthen national feeling after the war? There are no definitive answers to these questions.

Shortly before his death, the Brewer took stock of the political situation in Denmark in a letter to the poet and dramatist Holger Drachmann, but before we hear from the Brewer, it is important to recap on the history of Danish political parties. Although the constitution of 1849 had given Denmark its first democratic parliament, namely the Rigsdag, comprising the Folketing and the Landsting, there were still no parties. Votes were entrusted to individual persons.

Over time, however, Folketing members with the same political views began to meet in "clubs", which provided the platform for the formation of parties, which took place around 1870.

The "Right" was the name of the party now known as the Conservative People's Party, which back then consisted mainly of landowners and public servants. The "United Left" was the name of the modern Venstre (Left) Party, which consisted of farmers. These two parties comprised Folketing members who had already been elected.

The Social Democratic Party, which was established in 1871 and appealed to the workers, was founded outside the Rigsdag and did not acquire seats in the Folketing until the 1880s.

In the letter to Holger Drachmann, the Brewer declared his sympathy with the Right and attacked the Left, but maintained, as on other occasions, that he did not regard himself as being affiliated to any particular party and enjoyed the sovereignty of an individual politician:

"Fortunately, our constitution has introduced a genuine bicameral system (the best in Europe) which gives all classes of the population, i.e. the whole nation, equal rights and participation in the legislation but excludes cabinet collective responsibility, thereby safeguarding against the absolutism of a single class."

The Brewer cautioned against "mob absolutism" and saw the bicameral system as a safeguard against this. He concluded: "… how could one expect a nation which, in political terms, is wholly immature, to put it bluntly a child, to immediately understand how to use broad political power in the right way. After all, none of the European nations which have obtained free constitutions since the French Revolution have yet learnt this. I therefore believe in a happy future for Denmark, albeit I shall not experience it."

In the Brewer's eyes, this democratic development had to take place gradually. What are people supposed to do with freedom and democracy if they have not learnt how to use these privileges?

At the same time, the Brewer was convinced that a nation's unity depended on an unbroken historical line with the king as the unifying figure. The Brewer saw France as a horrific example in this regard.

"It is France's misfortune, under which it is still groaning, that in 1793 it severed its historical line by chopping off the head of the king."

The Brewer had experienced the war in 1864 and other wars in Europe in his lifetime, and he asserted that the air in Europe would continue to be full of "toxic infectious matter" for a long time to come. It was therefore a matter of Holger Drachmann and other poets, dramatists, popular speakers and authors girding their loins and taking part in the debate to "cleanse the spiritual atmosphere of all the toxic organisms or render them harmless, just as from Pasteur we have learnt to do in the physical world."

For the Brewer it was obvious that the nation's unity depended on a strong, unifying figure, namely the king, as well as a strong middle class which could assume political responsibility on behalf of the people. Democracy for all was something which had to come further down the road, insofar as the Brewer actually imagined that it could become a reality at all.

Because how could the Brewer have foreseen at that time that Denmark would end up with voting rights for women and servants, and that the Landsting would be abolished and cabinet collective responsibility introduced so that to this very day a Danish government cannot sit with a majority opposed to it?

The Brewer made do with asserting that he believed in a happy future for Denmark even if he would not be a part of it. And he maintained that democracy is something in which a nation needs to be educated.

In this he may have an important point given the situation in many turbulent parts of the world today where people are fighting for democracy and freedom: Denmark and other European nations had to go through much evil before democracy began to function in this particular corner of the world.

What exactly the Brewer meant by "cleanse the spiritual atmosphere" we cannot know for certain. But we can say that it was entirely natural for him to refer to science even in regard to something abstract.

The Brewer's own intellectual constitution – today we would speak of his values – was also characterised by this duality. The Brewer was a very down-to-earth and matter-of-fact person, but at the same time he was in possession of a non-dogmatic religious conviction which incorporated the thoughts and ideas of both Christianity and Antiquity.

When in 1887 he set off on his last journey to Rome, it was to be close to Antiquity and all its power and greatness for one last time.

CHAPTER 7: THE FINAL JOURNEY

It was cold in Rome when the Brewer arrived by train on 4 March 1887. He was accompanied by his wife Laura, his friend Sophie Steenstrup, and Agnes Berthelsen, affectionately called Auntie Berta, who over time had become the Brewer's private secretary. The party installed itself at Hotel Quirinale in the centre of Rome.

The Brewer had high expectations in every respect of what would turn out to be his final journey, to Rome, a city for which he cherished a great affection throughout his lifetime.

"Even from my childhood ancient Rome has thoroughly occupied my thoughts, and the rise and fortunes of the Romans have had such a predominant influence on the whole of the civilised world, and are in themselves so instructive, that my interest in Rome's history is still growing," the Brewer wrote to Johanne Louise Heiberg shortly before his departure.

There was, however, another reason for his high expectations. Carl was waiting for him in Rome with his wife Ottilia, completing the reconciliation process which had begun two years previously when Carl had offered the hand of reconciliation to his father. At that time he had sent a bouquet of flowers, delivered by his daughter Theodora to her grandparents. This was at Easter, and the Brewer, true to habit, was not slow in acknowledging the visit of his eldest grandchild in a short letter to Carl written on Easter Monday 1885:

"Thank you for the Easter greeting which you sent through Theodora, showing that you felt it would gladden me to see the innocent children and that you wish to grant me this joy in my old age. I see in this greeting a promise that for me also the long period of suffering can be superseded by a resurrection to a new and better life here on earth, and I can now sing with hope and confidence: 'Good Friday was a bitter day, but beautiful was Easter morn!'" The Brewer was referring to a much-loved hymn of the day penned by the Danish Romantic poet and playwright Adam Oehlenschläger.

This had been the first step in the two families re-establishing contact, and now it had been decided that they should take a trip together. Carl and Ottilia wanted to go to Greece on an archaeological tour together with a number of artists and scientists, but beforehand they would stop off in Rome and meet up with the Brewer and Laura.

Now they had all finally made it to Rome, even though initially Laura had refused to take part. She was not keen on the trip and said she felt unhappy at the thought of having to go. She considered herself wholly inadequately qualified and read in the history of Rome. But when the Brewer had issued a note of ultimatum – "This time I'm not travelling without you because I won't be travelling anymore" – she agreed to go, albeit with a strange premonition that something would happen.

The Brewer himself also seems to have had a hidden purpose for his long journey to Rome. He wanted to satisfy himself that everything could proceed as it should when he was "gone". Before his departure, he wrote to Johanne Louise Heiberg:

"Now that I have basically completed my many years of work building up and organising my brewery, I feel a need to consider the workings of the entire creation from a distance, and thereby, I hope, assure myself that everything can proceed as it should when I am gone. I therefore decided to take a very long trip, and so now in my seventy-sixth year I shall make a second visit to Rome, where I am certain that the time will not pass slowly as each day I shall be busy with mental and, if I have the energy, physical activity."

Endless sunshine

It is said that one goes to Rome to remember. Here among the ruins of Rome's glorious age the Brewer felt good. And he undoubtedly remembered a great deal.

Most certainly he thought back to his first visit to Rome twenty-five years previously with Carl. "We are enjoying endless sunshine," Carl had written home on that occasion, when father and son spent a whole seven weeks exploring Rome's rich history, which the Brewer knew by heart. Carl also recalled the "splendid sight" of his father riding around the square on a donkey.

Just as father and son had enjoyed discussing brewing, they had also enjoyed their time together on that trip to Rome. That was worth the Brewer remembering now in the twilight of his life, and it built a bridge over the many unhappy clashes which life had brought.

On 8 March the family celebrated the arrival in Rome in 1797 of the sculptor Bertel Thorvaldsen. This was a date which

Thorvaldsen, who ended up spending forty years in Rome, had himself celebrated as his "Roman birthday". This tradition was taken up by the Brewer, who was deeply fascinated by Thorvaldsen throughout his life and owned no less than thirty-two of his works.

The event was also attended by a number of Danes residing in Rome. They ate together at a trattoria which had been known over the years as a meeting place for international authors and artists. Here at the Falcone near Piazza Navona twenty-five years earlier the Brewer and Carl had met up with the Danish community in Rome, and both father and son had been members of the Scandinavian Society. Subsequently the Brewer often talked about his Roman friends.

ROSES FOR THORVALDSEN Bertel Thorvaldsen (1770-1844) is one of Denmark's greatest sculptors and, together with Antonio Canova and Johan Tobias Sergel, a leading light of Neoclassical sculpture.

In 1796 he travelled to Rome, where he lived and worked for the next forty years, punctuated by various journeys, including to Denmark. Thorvaldsen found a large audience in the cosmopolitan Rome and had contacts throughout Europe. When he returned home to Copenhagen in 1838 it was to great public interest. He became an honorary citizen of the city and acquired a home and studio at Charlottenborg. He died during a performance at the Royal Danish Theatre and is buried in the courtyard of Thorvaldsens Museum.

Throughout his lifetime the Brewer greatly revered the Danish sculptor, as was demonstrated many years after Thorvaldsen's death. Hans Christian Andersen wrote in his diary on Sunday 20 November 1870, which was the centenary of Thorvaldsen's birth:

"Went to Thorvaldsens Museum, which was packed with people; Thorvaldsen's former servant showed me that the biggest wreath was from Brewer Jacobsen, the beautiful rose garland, which people poured scorn on believing that they were artificial roses; it was really made up of large blooming roses and arrived by post in the morning from Hammerich." (*Thorvaldsen with Adam Oehlenschläger's bust,* painting by Johan Vilhelm Gertner, 1842. Thorvaldsens Museum. Photograph: Ole Woldbye)

FRIENDS IN ROME The Brewer was a child of the Romantic age, which dictated that any self-respecting artist in northern Europe simply had to make a journey to Rome. The interactions of Danish artists in Rome gradually became more organised following the setting up in 1833 of the Danish library. Norwegian and Swedish libraries were also established, and in 1860 the three libraries merged to form the Scandinavian Society of Artists and Scientists in Rome. It was this Society which the Brewer and his son visited when they were in Rome together for the first time in 1862, and the Brewer often talked about his "Roman friends".

The Brewer would undoubtedly have been delighted with this link between Rome and the Nordic countries, and it was in his spirit when in 1967 the Carlsberg Foundation donated a new building to the Danish Academy in Rome, a private institution under the Danish Ministry of Culture which provides a venue for research into art, culture and science. The Academy was founded in 1956 and has been housed since 1967 on the edge of the Villa Borghese park in the new building designed by the Danish architect Kay Fisker. Here, Danish researchers and artists can apply for residencies to work primarily in the areas of archaeology, philology, history, graphic art, architecture and music.

The Carlsberg Foundation provides funding through Queen Ingrid's Roman Fund. (*Danish artists at La Gensola Osteria in Rome* (Thorvaldsen in the foreground to the right), painting by Ditlev Blunck, 1837. Thorvaldsens Museum. Photograph: Hans Petersen)

A paradise on earth

Although the Brewer was delighted with Rome, it was Sorrento, south of Naples, which he once described to Johanne Louise Heiberg as "the only place I have stayed where I have not felt the need to work and have truly been able to give myself over to pleasure. This place has therefore etched itself into my memory as a paradise on earth".

On several occasions in his life the Brewer reflected that there was a world which he stood outside but which he longed for. A world where a person could give oneself over to pleasure and relaxation. In his case, this had only happened once, namely that time in Sorrento.

But this had not made the Brewer give up. He understood that he needed to compensate for what he could not manage himself by surrounding himself with people who had the character traits which he himself lacked:

"They are people in whose company I feel rejuvenated," he wrote to Carl in regard to some young acquaintances, "… and I need that because my temperament is not by nature lively enough, without help from outside, to give my spirit the flexibility with which its more weakly developed or crumbling predispositions can be sufficient for activity, whereby life itself first achieves its full, harmonic – as distinct from narrow – development."

The Brewer believed that the human spirit can be adapted if one consciously works at it. That was partly why he so frequently invited people to dinner parties and other gatherings at Carlsberg. On one such occasion he rebuked a guest who asserted that the Brewer had changed a lot at Carlsberg but had stayed the same in relation to his friends. According to a letter to Carl, the Brewer replied that the guest was mistaken:

"… because this too had changed inasmuch as now that

my busy work in practical life was diminishing and nearing its completion, I felt far more need than before *as a person* to associate with people, and specifically with those friends whose devotion could teach me to let myself go completely and undividedly, because therein I saw the greatest happiness."

In another letter to Carl, the Brewer touched upon the same subject. He wrote about his lack of satisfaction with himself – inwardly – and pointed to a solution which he had already begun to implement:

"… to try to forget what one is lacking, partly through strenuous activity – although this is slowly limited by physical vigour – and partly by remedying the lack by surrounding oneself with good, noble people who can nurture the seeds of goodness and gentleness, the spiritual and moral attributes in one which need to be cultivated in order for the person to be able to achieve the all-round development and perfection which are the goal of this earthly life."

And on yet another occasion the Brewer wrote:

"One must gather honey for one's hive from every flower."

Here the Brewer's entire understanding of the meaning of life is distilled down into one maxim. One must as a person continually strive for the greatest degree of perfection, among other things by seeking out people who are unlike oneself and tasks which seem, on the face of it, foreign. One must, he wrote to Carl, conquer one's disinclination or inertia "and not just desire but strive – upwards, always upwards in a moral and spiritual respect!"

The Brewer had an idealistic conception of being a human being, and he strove throughout his life to live up to this conception.

A PARADISE ON EARTH In the Brewer's time Sorrento was already a popular holiday destination due to its warm climate. The Brewer loved this "paradise on earth" probably because it was also close to historical sights such as Vesuvius, Pompeii, Amalfi and Herculaneum. (*Sorrento*, gouache by P. Lapira, 19th century. The Bridgeman Art Library. Photograph: Bonhams)

The greatest happiness

On the day of their arrival in Rome, the Brewer and the rest of the party were at the Roman Forum – the monumental square between the Palatine, Capitol and Esquiline Hills established from around 500 BCE as a venue for meeting, consultation and trade. It was not until five hundred years later, under Julius Caesar and Augustus, that the square acquired the form which it has today.

A SPECIAL PLACE When Johanne Louise Heiberg was residing in Rome in 1874 with the financial support of the Brewer, the Brewer wrote to her concerning the viewpoint in Rome which was for him "the most cherished of all".

"It is on the Palatine Hill, when one forces one's way over the ruins of the imperial palaces overgrown with shrubs and weeds out to the edge of the valley where Circus Maximus was situated. From some projecting points between the shrubs one has a wonderful view over the Tiber Valley to the heights on the other side and to St Peter's Church, whose dome presents itself in the most beautiful form, especially when the sun is setting behind it!" (*The Palatine Hill*, lithography by Godefroy Engelmann, 1850. Thorvaldsens Museum. Photograph: Helle Nanny Brendstrup)

The Brewer had arrived in Rome, and as usual there was no time to waste.

In those days, as he went around with his son and the rest of the family reacquainting himself with the place where, according to tradition, Romulus once built his house on a hill, later called the Palatine Hill, where all the later imperial rulers of Rome would live, he was certainly close to "the greatest happiness". The Palatine Hill was the Brewer's favourite place in Rome, he once revealed to Johanne Louise Heiberg.

The Brewer felt at home in this city, where he rediscovered the greatness and ruins of everything which had gone before: a large and powerful culture which had had a huge cultural and civilising influence on the world, but which nevertheless was now gone. Furthermore, he would now have the opportunity to enjoy everything one final time with Carl, who shared his father's enthusiasm for Rome. Carl would visit Italy no fewer than eighteen times during his lifetime, including Rome on nine occasions, usually to purchase antique objects.

A few days later, on 12 March, the Brewer was at the railway station to say farewell to Ottilia and Carl, who were moving on to Greece. Louis Pasteur's son and wife, who were residing in Rome, had also turned up to see them off.

Religious consciousness

The Brewer had probably heard of the novel *Corinne, ou l'Italie*, written in 1807 by the Swedish-French author Madame de Staël, who said of Rome: "Living in Rome is a gentle way of preparing oneself to die."

For a man whose watchword was self-activity, it must have been difficult to consider no longer being active. The Brewer had not made preparations for his own funeral, and there are only a handful of references in his letters to the end of life.

However, the death of the Danish pastor Just Henrik Voltelen Paulli in 1865 provided an occasion for the Brewer to give a detailed account of his religious conviction and his philosophy of life in a letter to Carl.

This spiritual testimony from the Brewer's own hand is an examination of the Christian church's dogmas, which the Brewer did not think much of. By contrast, he believed in an omnipotent God who leaves it up to individuals to live their lives in the best possible way. Although the Brewer reserved the right to a non-dogmatic faith, he did have a firm belief in eternal life. Otherwise, the Brewer believed, human life would be "sheer unreasonableness".

Church dogmas were too much for an independent mind such as the Brewer's, and he was not generally enamoured with the church as an institution. Nanna wrote:

"Here at Carlsberg God's word and God himself are rarely the subject of discussion. I do not think they lack faith – least of all Auntie, who is humble and in possession of precisely the right childlike faith – Uncle likes to see visitors here on Sundays, so Sunday morning is taken up with lots of other things. He never goes to church himself – he is too much of a rationalist to feel edified by a pastor's sermon. He believes in God as the ruler and creator – but I think he overlooks Christ. This is certainly quite common in our time! This is not the case, however, with Carl, though he seldom goes to church."

Later, however, Carl became an "ever attentive churchgoer" with an "innate fear of God", as his pastor Henry Ussing described it.

THE BREWER'S SPIRITUAL TESTAMENT

J.C. Jacobsen believed in God. But he did not have a dogmatic view of the nature of God. In a letter to Carl, the Brewer gave a highly detailed account of what he called his "religious consciousness", which was crucial to his "philosophy of life":

"I do not wish to be your religious instructor but to convey to you *my* religious consciousness as it has gradually evolved in me. The Protestant is not, like the Catholic, a *blind* believer, but his belief should be the result of his own testing and scrutiny. The Protestant does not believe because the pastor maintains this or that, but rather he considers what he has heard and read in the Bible and subsequently forms his *philosophy of life*. The Protestant community or "church" does not therefore constitute a "single entity" as does the Catholic community, in which the Pope alone has the right and authority to say what *must* be believed. In Protestants, self-activity in the individual in the sphere of belief is a *right* – and a *duty* – and the individual's belief therefore acquires a more or less individual character. For me almost everything which is called *dogma* is something unimportant, both contrary to reason and foreign to the true essence of Christianity. Part of that is nothing more than oriental ideas, myths and figurative language which were assimilated by the earliest Christian fathers of the church into the "holy scriptures". I do not understand the doctrine of the trinity, but in my view Christianity does not need this nimbus to substantiate its divine origin. The doctrine of the atonement seems to me to be contrary to reason, and I believe in it as little as I do the trinity. That all the people who lived before Christ and all those living afterwards who, through no fault of their own, are ignorant of the morals of Christianity should be condemned to hell is in my view an utterly unchristian doctrine. That none here in this world can be so perfect, and thus so fortunate, as those who know and follow the true teaching, *this is truth*, but inasmuch as there is a life after this one in which the conditions for a higher perfection prevail, in so much can their imperfection also not last *eternally*.

But if I discount such important dogmas as those mentioned above, what then remains in the way of dogmas in which I do believe. I believe in one God who created the world, which in every respect bears the marks of and testifies to a wisdom, for which reason human beings must bow in humility and awe. By the world I not only understand the earth and all the other planets which move through space, but also the spiritual life which moves through time: human life. Here too the eternal wisdom makes itself apparent as being infinitely high above humanity's short-sighted insight such that *humanity*, in spite of all the mistakes of individuals, in spite of apparent or real, but transient, regressions, is nevertheless advancing to a higher existence, so that truth and rationality, in spite of fallacy and wickedness, are still slowly but surely prevailing. *This for me is God's providence*. I do not believe in the *special* providence which the individual invokes in a given situation because this belief, as beautiful and consoling as it is, contradicts reason and goes against belief in a rational *world order* (see Oersted's writings).

All the same, because I do not believe that God, at the individual's *petition*, intervenes in the world order or performs miracles, I do not consequently fail to appreciate the *petition*, the warm, humble, deep approach to the supreme being, but I only attach value to the petition insofar as the goal of the petitioner's desire is to be strengthened in wisdom, patience, humility, and so forth.

But now to the doctrine of immortality! Is it possible to philosophically prove its truth? No! Can we comprehend immortality? No, as little as we here on earth, as finite beings, can comprehend in any way the infinite in time or space. Should I then believe in what I cannot comprehend, let alone prove the veracity of?

My answer is an unconditional yes! For without immortality the whole of human life seems to me to be sheer unreasonableness. Without immortality there would be *no* eternal *justice* because the wicked are carried away suddenly without receiving their punishment and the good similarly without receiving their reward. Next: it seems clear to me that the whole of human life necessarily requires a continuation beyond death. It is impossible that humans could have acquired a divine spark in their inner being solely to eat, drink, sleep and die. *The goal of the human being is spiritual and moral perfection.* The obtaining thereof is *salvation*, failure leads to repentance, pain, infernal torment. This is how we figuratively refer to God's judgement, God's grace. But this strong desire for perfection cannot, as we see, be satisfied here on earth and many are taken away at an early age, even as small children. Was there any reason in such an existence without a continuation beyond the grave? No! So there must be a *continuation*, and with *awareness* of the life lived down here. Of this I think there can be not the slightest doubt. Speculation on the *form* of the continued life is of no use as our thinking cannot penetrate eternity. It is not easy to resist the temptation to let the imagination visualise this state of existence, but we should not dwell too much on it, and at all times remain clear in our minds that it is only imagination and not thought which calls forth these images. Because then life here on earth is of no importance." [Italics are the Brewer's, ed.]

Decline in Rome

When the weather in Rome remained unsettled after Carl and Ottilia had moved on to Greece, the Brewer considered for a while whether the party should head further south to Sorrento. But his innate resistance to changing plans led him to remain with Laura and the two ladies and wait for better weather. Instead, he began to fall ill in the spring chill of Rome, where the temperature was a mere seven to nine degrees.

On Saturday 26 March the Brewer suffered an asthma attack. He got out of bed at four o'clock in the morning, grabbed his German Baedecker guidebook and staggered out into the city to find a doctor. As well as asthma, he had bad pains in his stomach and was unable to pass water.

His critical condition did not stop him following his principle of self-activity and he did manage to see a German doctor, Dr Neuhaus, who escorted him to a bath house and administered massage, but it did not help. He was then sent to bed in the hotel with warm blankets and drops to help with the asthma.

On the Sunday morning Dr Neuhaus sent for Professor Duranti, a surgeon. He came to the hotel with his assistant, Dr Cami, and they inserted a catheter, which immediately improved the Brewer's condition. But this was not enough. The Brewer had a problem with his prostate and required an operation.

This was followed by a long period of convalescence, but it did not bring about a recovery. The doctors saw the Brewer every day, and Agnes Berthelsen kept watch day and night over "our dear old darling".

The Brewer himself did what he could: every day he drank half a bottle of his friend Gabriel Sedlmayr's beer and ate anchovies, which he loved and which were obtained for him in the city. In his fevered state he also managed to take care of some business. Among other things, on 10 April he dictated a letter to the architectural painter Heinrich Hansen concerning a fountain at Frederiksborg and only made brief mention of his illness.

"I am unwell and must remain in bed, though the illness is not perilous."

Perilous or not, the symptoms of the illness fluctuated back and forth.

One evening the Brewer said to Laura: "We two old people have come to Rome, and it may seem crazy, but I have enjoyed the 4th and the 8th with Carl, and that makes up for everything."

The Brewer was referring to the fact that he himself arrived in Rome on 4 March and Thorvaldsen arrived in Rome on 8 March, which was the day when the family always celebrated Thorvaldsen's Roman birthday. The Brewer continued:

"I looked deep into his soul, which I would not perhaps have had the opportunity to do at home, and everything else is of minor importance."

Of course I know you, Carl

The worst thing apart from dying is dying far from home. But not in the case of Rome. The Brewer considered it everything that he had enjoyed the 4th and the 8th with Carl. This was possibly a slightly cryptic way of saying that for him there was a rebirth, a new birthday, associated with arriving in the Eternal City. Father and son had been reborn together. And this had drawn death's sting.

A month had now passed in which the Brewer's condition had steadily declined and in which Laura and the two ladies probably took turns watching over the Brewer. Finally, Carl and Ottilia were summoned and arrived in Rome on 30 April 1887 at six o'clock in the morning.

When Carl and Ottilia entered the hotel room, the Brewer was very ill and in a state of delirium.

"I had the thought that I would have preferred not to see him like this," Carl wrote in his memoirs.

It is said that a person dies as he or she has lived, and so it was with the Brewer. He was a strong-willed man who fought to the very end to maintain control.

The Brewer had always said to Carl: "Help yourself and God will help you." Now the Brewer could no longer help himself, so what would happen now?

Carl wrote about the Brewer's final hours:

"I tried several times to find a lucid moment. 'Do you not know me, father?' 'Of course I know you, Carl' or similar. But after a few coherent words he began to talk about French verbs and other such things.

"Once he began to talk about the 'agreement' in an almost angry tone. Each time I said, 'You must be suffering a lot,' he would quickly reply, 'No, not in the least.'

"Indeed, I do not think his suffering on that final day was particularly great, but I am also sure that his reply only really meant that he would not admit it even if he were suffering.

"A bit later, around ten or eleven o'clock, there was a more lucid moment. I asked: 'Father, are you pleased to see me.' He answered very clearly … (He made a gesture with his hands as if to embrace me) 'How can you ask that? Of course I'm pleased to see you.'

"I said: 'I didn't think when I said goodbye to you at the railway station that I would see you again so ill.'

"He then said that it was the greatest – he sought for the word – event – joy that we had been together, and it was clear that this was what he was really thinking, but then he began talking deliriously again.

"I bought some roses, presented them to him and held them up to his nose. He only said, 'They don't smell,' and didn't seem to care for them. When the others said to him, 'It's roses that Carl's giving you,' he said, 'Thank you,' and looked at me in a friendly way. He then groped for them and put his hand on them. I then said to him, 'You really don't know how ill you are.' He looked up and quickly said, 'What do you mean by that.' 'You're very ill, much worse than you think.' But this time he didn't reply.

"I wept bitterly, but that didn't seem to affect him. I read the Lord's blessing over him as I held his head, but I don't think he took any notice of this either."

At midday the Brewer was sat up in bed and briefly recognised the doctor. Carl then said the Lord's prayer for him, without him seeming to notice.

As the time approached two o'clock in the afternoon, the Brewer became weaker. Carl and Ottilia were alone with him at this point, and Carl was holding his right hand in his. Carl wrote:

"Just before the moment of death his head sank to the left, where Ottilia was standing, and his eyes fell upon her with an expression of recognition. This was the final impression he received in his life. I bent down over him to perhaps also receive a look, but he then drew his final shallow breath."

It was 30 April 1887, just after two o'clock in the afternoon: Captain J.C. Jacobsen, the Brewer, was dead.

Farewell from the Brewer

Later that afternoon Carl took a walk. He wandered to the Capitoline Hill past the Forum Romanum, the Colosseum and the Arch of Constantine, then back past the Forum Romanum and over the Capitoline Hill to the Pantheon and the Corso. He visited the Piazza Monte d'Oro and the house where his father and he had stayed twenty-five years previously, and he tried to find the restaurant where they had eaten.

"It was essentially the same walk he and I had taken 25 years before on that first evening in Rome," Carl wrote.

With this walk, Carl was saying farewell to Rome from the Brewer.

The Brewer's body was laid in a wooden coffin "lined and surrounded with white cloth", as Carl wrote. The coffin was fetched at four o'clock on the Sunday morning, presumably so as not to rouse the attention of the hotel's other guests, and driven to the chapel of the Protestant Cemetery in Rome. Carl remained standing, watching the hearse drive away from the hotel.

On Tuesday 3 May a service was held at the chapel of the Protestant Cemetery before the coffin was dispatched to Copenhagen.

Carl and Ottilia, together with Laura and the two ladies, continued their journey and only reached Carlsberg shortly before the coffin arrived.

The coffin arrived at Copenhagen's railway station on Thursday 19 May. Brewery workers from Old Carlsberg had assembled to carry the coffin to the hearse, which drove it to the chapel of the Church of Holmen.

On Saturday 21 May the coffin was driven to Carlsberg, where it was placed in Pompeii, the winter garden with peristyle which the Brewer had built and of which he was so proud. Here a service was held for all the Carlsberg employees after the coffin had been adorned with silver wreaths and flowers.

The funeral

The funeral took place on Monday 23 May at Copenhagen's cathedral, the Church of Our Lady.

The Brewer's coffin was driven in cortège from Pompeii to the cathedral. Behind the hearse walked Carl with his seven-year-old son Alf.

FAREWELL TO THE BREWER After J.C. Jacobsen's death in Rome, his body was taken to Pompeii at Carlsberg to give the brewery employees an opportunity to say farewell. From there the coffin was taken to the Church of Our Lady, where the funeral took place and where the coffin was placed in the chapel. In 1891, when Carl Jacobsen had completed the Jesus Church in Valby, J.C. Jacobsen was finally laid to rest here. (Carlsberg Archive)

Carl, who had made all the arrangements for the funeral, had chosen the cathedral as the venue. The Brewer would no doubt have approved. The cathedral, which had been destroyed during the English bombardment in 1807, had been rebuilt in the Greco-Roman classical style by the architect Christian Frederik Hansen in 1829. The adornments had been provided by the sculptors Bertel Thorvaldsen, Herman Vilhelm Bissen and Jens Adolf Jerichau, all leading names whom the Brewer had held in high honour.

Here, under Thorvaldsen's marble statue of Saint Peter with the keys to Heaven and the statues of the other eleven apostles, the Brewer's coffin now stood. In the pews sat King Christian IX together with a large congregation, including representatives of science, culture and politics.

The funeral was conducted by Christen Ewaldsen, the pastor of Frederiksberg Church. He had formerly been a pastor in the parish of St Nicholas in Flensburg, in the disputed Schleswig region, and had been preferred over the German pastors in Schleswig after 1864. He would later bury Carl's children.

It would undoubtedly have gladdened the Brewer that standing now by his coffin was a man who in his own way had fought for the cause of the Danes. And in fact the pastor began by referring to the Brewer's importance for the fatherland:

"The fact that in this hour the nation's king and so many of its finest men are here assembled in the funeral congregation around this coffin is fully warranted because our beloved fatherland has lost one of its best sons. And he was a loving son to this mother, beneath the greying hairs he loved her with all the warmth of youth; he fully appropriated the tenet that one owes everything to one's fatherland, yet he had not just learnt it by heart but incorporated it into his life, and great monuments will bear witness to the coming generations of this his filial devotion."

The pastor also talked of the Brewer's relationship to work:

"He was a working man like few others; but for him work was not a task which was imposed on him, a duty with which he was burdened, it was the very pulse beat of his life, the air which he needed to breathe, for him living and working merged into one... But however much he loved work, he was never a slave to it because he was always a head taller than the task and could therefore handle it with serenity and with a sure hand let it be his servant. This came from the fact that he became acquainted early with two high-born friends, art and science, whom he offered lodgings in his heart, and they had taken up the offer and, as befits two such noble siblings, lived peacefully together in him. However, he did not regard himself as their landlord who gave them shelter or had the right to demand anything from them, he only wished to sit as a disciple at their feet, listen to what they had to say and thereby grow steadily in serenity."

The defeat in 1864 was also mentioned in the sermon:

"Among the many wreaths on his coffin there is one from North Schleswig, and it is well deserved because no more genuine, loyal friend has this our grieving land had here at home, and few things could vex him more than when he encountered the faint-hearted and dispirited talk which abandoned hope and could only dwell on the language of the lost Schleswig. Perhaps it was our agreement on this point which led him to grant me insight into what resided in his heart."

Finally, reference was also made to the Brewer's final days, including an indirect reference to the reconciliation between father and son:

"... those closest to him will never forget the final time

THE BREWER'S FINAL RESTING PLACE The Jacobsen family's sarcophagi stand in the crypt beneath the Jesus Church, which was built as a mausoleum and is one of Denmark's most distinctive churches.

The Jesus Church, which was designed by the architect Vilhelm Dahlerup and commissioned by Carl Jacobsen, is a richly furnished cathedral. Carl Jacobsen effected the fitting out of a church which left nothing wanting in terms of grandeur and magnificence.

Carl, who was described as a free-thinker, also incorporated a number of unconventional elements in the church which his contemporaries deemed blasphemous. In particular, the erection outside the church of the sculptor Niels Hansen Jacobsen's figure *Troll that smells Christian blood* caused a sensation. But as Carl said: "Satan wants to get his claws into you, so you must look to God and attend church." The figure was subsequently moved and erected elsewhere.

The most prominent message in the Jesus Church is the phrase "You are the Christ", which is painted on the arch leading into the altar chamber.

The distinctive church interior can perhaps be seen as a departure from the Brewer's understanding of Christianity, which only involved belief in Yahweh and the Old Testament with its laws and commandments. Jesus Christ and the Holy Spirit were not part of the Brewer's creed.

Carl, who like his father did not allow himself to be labelled in relation to his faith, was extremely god-fearing. However, he appears to have focused primarily on the New Testament and Christ as saviour. The Brewer found his final resting place under the Jesus Church, where Simon Peter's reply to Jesus when Jesus asked his disciples who he was stands proud: "You are the Christ. The son of the living God." (Scanpix. Photograph: Brian Bergmann) they spent with him, when every cloud was blown away such that the moment of his passing was like the sun going down in the clear light of an autumn evening."

The final word

From his sickbed in Rome the Brewer had written to the architectural painter Heinrich Hansen concerning the restoration of the Neptune Fountain, which the Swedes had removed from Frederiksborg Castle in 1659 during the storming of Copenhagen.

Over a long period the Brewer had put much effort into reconstructing the large fountain in the outer castle yard, and with ministerial intervention he had obtained permission from the Swedish king to make casts from the original, which was to be found in Drottningholm Castle in Stockholm. The Brewer had himself been to Sweden to inspect the work, and he had made a copy of the fountain, which had been erected at Carlsberg, where he had conducted trials with the path of the jets based on ingenious calculations.

"Uncle Jacobsen is, as you know, always to be found here, there and everywhere, but right now he is even a master of the water jets," wrote Johannes Steenstrup the year before the Brewer's death.

Politically there was a lot of opposition to the fountain project. But as usual the Brewer had made refusal almost impossible by providing both practically and financially for everything in connection with the fountain's restoration at Frederiksborg Castle. And providence ordained that the Danish authorities said yes to the costly gift around the very time when the Brewer closed his eyes for the last time in Rome.

The Brewer was dead. Yet he had the final say, just as he had been accustomed to throughout his long, productive life.

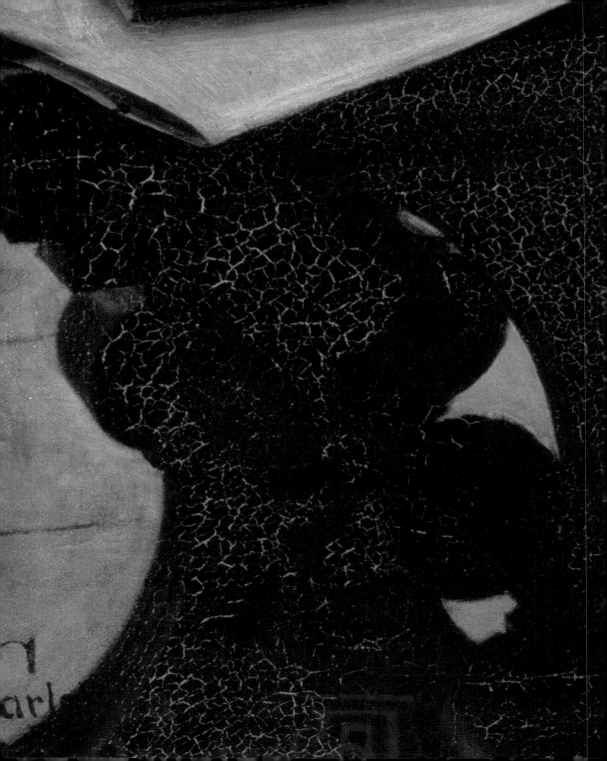

EPILOGUE: A HOMAGE TO BEER

It is said that beer was discovered through misfortune. Witty minds have observed that the real misfortune was that it was not discovered sooner.

It is indeed true that it was chance which led our ancestors to begin brewing beer, probably around ten thousand years ago. And ever since then human beings have been drinking the golden nectar. In 2010, one hundred and eighty-five billion litres of beer were consumed globally, and the Danes drank their share, averaging ninety litres of beer per capita. We drink beer with food. We drink beer on the terrace on a hot summer's day. We drink beer when we watch football. And we drink beer at funerals. We have also begun to drink more expensive quality beers when we need something more special. In recent years, the Copenhagen restaurant Noma, recipient of the San Pellegrino Best Restaurant in the World award in both 2010 and 2011, and the acclaimed Danish chef Claus Meyer have been leading the way by championing connoisseur beers as an alternative to wine with exquisite gourmet food.

As the Danish cartoonist and humorist Robert Storm Petersen, known more commonly by his pen name Storm P, famously said: "Life is wonderful, but there's nothing like a large glass of well-poured beer!" Lauding it even more highly, if that were possible, the Danish comedy duo Monrad and Rislund sang "Beer is god". "Beer is proof that God loves us and wants us to be happy," opined Benjamin Franklin, the American statesman, inventor and scientist.

The magic potion

First and foremost, however, beer is a product which has been part and parcel of the human experience for a very long time.

It is an established fact that women have been the instigators of so much in human history, and the first beer brewer in the world was in all probability … a breweress. There are no references to that momentous occasion, but we are at liberty to assume that it was closely bound up with grain growing in one of the first agricultural societies in the Middle East. Back then, when humans made the transition from nomadic hunters to settled farmers, women took on the domestic chores. Various types of grain quickly became the basis for baking bread, and these women first became privy to the mysteries of fermentation. At some later point, almost certainly by chance, a woman may well have left some gruel standing around and discovered that fermentation could not only conjure up volume in bread but also conjure up a drink which tasted good.

From the Sumerians, who lived in Mesopotamia, present-day Iraq, we have our first written testimony to the magical power of beer. In the *Epic of Gilgamesh*, written in cuneiform script some three thousand years before the common era and regarded as the world's first literary work, we hear of the wild man Enkidu, who was primitive and dumb until he was offered beer to drink:

"Enkidu drank seven cups of beer and his heart soared. In this condition he washed himself and became a human being."

It should be no surprise to learn that it was a woman, the bearer of the mighty primal force which can give birth to children and brew beer, who offered Enkidu the beer which made him a human being.

When the Babylonians inherited power, they also inherited the Sumerian experiences of beer brewing. The Babylonians knew how to brew no less than twenty different types of beer. But not beer as we know it today. Rather, a cloudy, unfiltered drink which was often drunk through a tube with a filter on the end to avoid getting the bitter, fermented grain residues in the mouth. King Hammurabi, who was responsible for one of the earliest known collections of laws in the world in around 1780 BCE, also legislated on beer: an ordinary worker in Babylon was to receive a ration of two litres of beer a day, while high-ranking officials and priests were to receive five litres.

Later on, a genuine beer culture developed in Egypt with large breweries and great variation in the brewing process. Beer was brewed for the households of the pharaohs, priests and nobles, and large quantities for the workers on the pyramids. The scribes in Egypt created a new hieroglyph for the word "brewer", and dead Egyptians were provided with beer in their graves as an offering.

From grave-reliefs we know the precise method which the Egyptians used to brew beer. Firstly, the grain was transported to the brewery, where it was pounded to separate the chaff from the grain. Next, the cleaned grain was ground in a mill and sieved. The flour was then kneaded with water and formed into loaves, which were baked. When it came time for brewing, the loaves were broken into pieces, softened and pressed into pots. Water was added, and fermentation proceeded until the desired "loaf beer" was obtained. Today, the beer known as *buza* is still made according to this recipe.

The Greeks and Romans also brewed beer. However, the Romans regarded beer as a Barbarian drink and it was only brewed on the fringes of the empire, where it was difficult to obtain wine.

The Egtved Bronze Age Girl

As agriculture spread from the fertile regions of Asia Minor up through Europe, beer came with it. The first real evidence of beer brewing in Danish antiquity also has to do with the cult of the dead and a woman. What is more, a woman about whom we actually know a little bit. The Egtved Girl, named after the village in Southern Denmark where she was found, was only young when she died on a summer's day around 1370 BCE. In the Bronze Age barrow where she was chanced upon during an excavation in 1921, at her feet lay a small bucket made of birch bark. The thick brown deposit at the bottom of the bucket was the remains of a fermented drink made of grain, berries and honey with various added spices.

The Egtved Girl died at about the same time as another well-known woman was born in ancient Egypt: Queen Nefertiti, the most important wife of Pharaoh Amenhotep IV. The fact that the two women nourished themselves with roughly the same drink is a fascinating thought. However, there is so much that we do not know. Not least, was it actually beer which they were drinking in the Bronze Age? Or was it mead, a fermented drink based on honey?

It is not all that remarkable that in most cultures beer has been associated with a certain magic. Its genesis is more than a little amazing. You mix grain and water, leave it to ferment, and then you have a drink which quenches the thirst. But more than that, it also induces a measure of euphoria in the drinker. It is this effect which has conferred on beer, and indeed all alcoholic drinks, a mythical status: a wealth of rites and gods have surrounded beer throughout the ages.

In Norse mythology, Freya was the goddess of love and fertility who also provided the harvest, and hence beer. In particular, the Eddic poems *The Prophecy of the Seeress* and *The Ballad of Grimnir* make reference to both beer and mead, with no clear distinction between the two.

The Norse people, like the Romans, probably regarded wine as slightly finer than beer. Not least, of course, because wine was often difficult to obtain as it was produced far to the south. In a price-list from Bergen (present-day Norway) from 1306, the wine for a party of fifty-four people cost the same as a farm! Hence there is also strong symbolic value in the fact that Odin only drinks wine: "But on wine alone the weapon-glorious Odin aye liveth."

The other gods, by contrast, drank beer and mead. Thor, for example, the son of Odin and Freya, drained three large tankards of mead at the somewhat extraordinary wedding feast of the giant Thrym. And in general the Norse gods and goddesses (the Æsir) demanded beer: "Let the beer for the Aesir flow!" rang out the cry. Beer and mead were also the preferred drink of both giants and men.

The higher powers were also associated with beer following the introduction of Christianity. The Catholics have a wealth of saints reputed to protect beer and brewing, which are still revered in many Catholic countries today.

THE NORSEMEN DRINK TILL THEY DROP "As soon as they wake up – and they often sleep well into the day – they wash, usually in hot water because their winter lasts most of the year. Having washed, they eat a meal. They sit separately, each at their own table. Armed, they then set off on their business or – just as often – to party. They see no shame in drinking day and night. As is common among those who become drunk, there are frequent quarrels, which are rarely settled with cursing alone, but more often with killing and wounding.

"For drink they have a liquid which is made from barley or wheat and fermented so that it is somewhat akin to wine. Those who live closest to the Rhine also buy wine. Their food is simple and consists of wild fruits, unhung game and junket. With no finer repast and without the addition of spices, they dispel their hunger. But towards thirst they do not show the same moderation. If one indulges them in their drunkenness and fetches them all they demand, they will succumb far more easily to this load than to force of arms." (Extract from Publius Cornelius Tacitus: *Concerning the geography, the manners, the customs and the tribes of Germany*) (*Tap-room*, drawing by Lorenz Frølich, 1895. Carlsberg Archive)

The Nordic love of beer

From the Roman historian Tacitus we know a little more about the Nordic beer culture. The Norsemen, it would seem, had no qualms about sitting and drinking day and night. And at times it was beer rather than weaponry which proved their undoing.

It is popular mythology that the Norsemen were over-fond of their drink, but there is something in it. After all, how else would they while away the long winter days and nights if not eating, drinking and having a good time around the fire? It was rather different here to life under more southerly skies, where the warmth and wine invited an altogether different food and drink culture.

Beer and mead remained the symbol of Nordic power and strength. The Vikings said "skol" ("cheers", literally "cup") and duly passed the cup around. There was great hospitality in Viking homes, and fortunate was the woman who acquired the nickname "Alugod" (from the words "beer" and "good"), which attested that she was an excellent breweress and that her home was worth visiting.

Beer from the abbeys

In the Middle Ages beer made its ultimate breakthrough in Europe, not least to the credit of monks. As a rich abbey culture arose throughout Europe, knowledge and experience were accumulated beyond national borders, including in relation to the art of beer brewing. The abbey beer was brewed in three forms. The lowest-quality beer was given to the poor and pilgrims, the good beer was undoubtedly reserved for persons of rank and other guests at the abbey, and the moderate beer was presumably drunk by the monks themselves.

In Denmark, abbeys were established from around 1100. Here, they gathered top yeast for the brewing process, which was the only method known at that time. In the abbey gardens, the monks grew medicinal plants for treating sickness, including hops, which have a range of healing properties but were also used together with other spices to brew the beer.

Abbey life came to an abrupt end in northern Europe with the Reformation, which culminated in Denmark in 1536. Yet Katharina von Bora, the former nun who married the reformer Martin Luther, ran both a farm and a brewery after their marriage. Beer would continue to be brewed, Reformation or no Reformation.

In Denmark there were one hundred and forty abbeys before the Reformation. Today, just a few remain. In some places in Europe, however, the abbeys continue the tradition of brewing beer. Among others, the Trappists in Belgium and the Netherlands still brew and sell the traditional Trappist beer, which is brewed within the abbey walls by monks themselves.

Men take up the noble art

It was also during the Middle Ages that cities began to emerge, and with them the first beerhouses, or pubs as we would now call them, where visitors could pay to enjoy a beer. As beer became a commodity, the Crown began to tax it, and the need arose for specialist brewers who could ensure the quality of the beer.

The fact that beer could now be traded had a number of consequences. Whereas previously brewers had often been women, brewing now became a predominantly male profession. Production began to be systematised, and brewers' guilds were established. In 1525 the first brewers' guild was founded in Copenhagen, which was home to the majority of artisan brewers.

At the same time, Danish beer was under pressure. During the sixteenth and seventeenth centuries, untold barrels of beer came in over the border from the German Hanseatic cities. The

WITH MOTHER AT HOME The author and songwriter Jeppe Aakjær (1866-1939) recalls how his mother used to brew beer:

"Then mother began with her never-failing ingenuity to brew the home's beer. For me it always had an especially good taste, not least the Christmas beer. Mother's work with the beer brewing was always a mystery for us children, except of course for the one of us, my eldest sister, who was let into the secret.

"It was a great favour for a man, big or small, to be called to the back door, half of which could be pushed back against the wall, and to be allowed to taste the wort in mother's ladle. I watched father stand there on many occasions, a gentle look in his eyes, and with a jest take mother's ladle in the half-door. He could look at his wife so lovingly at those times.

"O childhood days, how rich you are in the memory! In my mind I can still smell mother's beer at the brewer's door." (Extract from Jeppe Aakjær's *Mother's workday. Portraits of peasant life in the seventies*, drawing, 1933. Carlsberg Archive)

Det bajerske Øl brygges.

HOW TO BREW BEER The drawing depicts the Brewer and Carl brewing Bavarian beer, and specifically stirring the contents of a mash tun. The drawing was produced by an unknown artist on the occasion of New Carlsberg's twenty-fifth anniversary in 1905.

Brewing beer now is not as simple as depicted here.

Beer is an alcoholic drink produced by a brewing process using water and yeast plus malt, typically from barley. Malt is the grain-based substance which is produced when the grain is made to germinate, after which the germination is halted before the grain really begins to grow, which usually takes place after five days.

Malting and mashing, in which the grain's starch is converted to fermentable sugars, are followed by separation of the wort, which is the sugar-containing liquid which is subsequently fermented into beer.

The wort is boiled and has various spices added, in particular hops, which counter the beer's sweetness and give a slightly bitter and aromatic flavour. Finally, a yeast is added to the wort, which converts the wort's sugar to alcohol and carbonic acid.

Top fermentation takes place between fifteen and thirty degrees, which gives a rapid fermentation. When the fermentation is complete, the yeast is found at the top of the beer, hence "top fermentation" and "top yeast". Top yeast is used for ales, wheat beer and traditional stouts and porters. Wine is also produced by top fermentation.

Bottom fermentation takes place between five and ten degrees, which means that it takes longer than top fermentation. When the fermentation is complete, the yeast is found at the bottom of the beer, hence "bottom fermentation" and "bottom yeast". Lager beers are bottom-fermented. (Drawing, Carlsberg Archive)

German beer, brewed from wheat with added hops, was a big hit in Denmark. Although hefty duties had to be paid, the German beer was a serious competitor to the Danish beer, at least for those who had the money. The man in the street was increasingly having to make do with distilled spirits and low-alcohol white beer. Later on, Bavarian beer, or "lager" as it came to be known, would arrive in Denmark and make quite an impact.

Country beer

In the countryside, however, it was still the women who were largely responsible for producing home-brewed beer right up to the end of the nineteenth century, when the industrially produced, bottom-fermented beer took over. On the farms, where the bulk of Denmark's beer originated, the brewing was carried out in a small brewhouse under the expert guidance of the farmer's wife based on experience accumulated over generations.

Country beer was top-fermented and brewed in several forms. It included an everyday beer brewed whenever the barrel was running dry, and special festive beer, which was drunk at Christmas, Easter, Whitsun and other festivals.

Brewing beer was a lengthy process. First, the grain had to be carried down from the loft and poured into the steeping tank, which stood in the yard alongside the well. Then the tank was filled with water and grain, after which the steep was monitored for several days. This was the first step in the malting.

When the grain had softened to a satisfactory extent, the steep was carried up to the germinating loft to germinate. Here it was a tough job keeping the temperature at the right level to control the germination process. If the grain became too cold, it had to be warmed by piling it up. And if it became too warm, the piles had to be spread out and aerated.

After several days, the germination was interrupted and

the malt dried to a greater or lesser extent depending on what type of malt was desired. This could be done by the kitchen fireplace or oven. After this, the malted grain could be stored until the brewing was to take place.

On the day of brewing, the copper was heated and all the tools were thoroughly scalded. The slightest impurity could give the beer a bad taste. The malted grain was poured into the vat and hot water poured over for mashing-in.

Subsequently, the softened malt was ladled out into a brewing vat, which was placed on a tripod, and boiling water was poured over the top. In the bottom of the brewing vat was a hole, which was plugged with a pin. A bundle of rye-straw was laid in the vat and held in place with hot stones. This functioned as a sieve when the wort was later drained from the vat by lifting the pin.

The first drawing was the strongest. This was the "storage beer". It was important to take time with each drawing. The water needed to be thoroughly boiled before being poured onto the malt, and the malt needed to be allowed to infuse so that the strength was removed from the grains. It was said that "a long brewing and a lazy brewer produce the best beer".

Next, the hops needed to be added, and finally the most important thing: the fermentation.

Fresh yeast was scarce, so dried yeast had to be used from the previous brewing as in previous times, which often produced a dubious result. Perhaps that is why they often resorted to incantations and superstition. In his novel *O.T.*, Hans Christian Andersen described the farm women screaming, laughing and dancing jacketless around the beer vat in the brewery and tossing in a silver coin. This was supposed to make the beer stronger and more intoxicating.

When fermentation was complete, the beer was poured into clean barrels. It was then ready to be drunk after a few days.

Beer for the new-born

Beer played an important role in life's rites of passage in the countryside, beginning with the birth of a new child. It is recounted that midwives in western Jutland offered the new-born baby bread, beer and distilled spirits as a type of superstitious act to ensure that the child would never lack these things.

Beer was also drunk at weddings, which generally extended over several days. The wedding was only at an end when the wedding toast had been made.

The Danish word for wake translates literally as "grave beer", which makes perfect sense when one hears how beer has been drunk at Danish funerals within the last two hundred years.

In western Zealand people recall how they used to turn up in the morning before a funeral, which would take place at the church in the afternoon. The guests would congregate in the drawing room, where the dead body was placed, usually on the dining table. The men drank schnapps, while the women drank beer with a rusk. The funeral was often followed by several days of partying.

Partying aside, whatever the occasion, beer also had an everyday purpose. There was little access to clean water, and in many cases beer was consumed to quench the thirst and/or allay hunger. A typical nineteenth-century Danish breakfast comprised beer, bread and bacon. As Professor C. Olufsen wrote in 1812 in *Instructions for the Peasantry on the Brewing of Beer*:

"Good beer is not just a healthy, nourishing and pleasant drink: it may well be the only thing which the inhabitants of the northern lands have in proper quantity and quality."

Clean drinking water was a scarce commodity, and the water used for brewing beer was disinfected by boiling to render it safe. The top-fermented white beer which was drunk in Denmark also happened to be rich in nutrients, which explains why the Danes drank it as we would drink water, tea and coffee today.

A new beer on the scene

In less than a hundred years, however, the attitude to beer would have changed completely, as attested to by a woman from one of the Danish islands:

"In the eighties [1880s, ed.] lager beer began to get fashionable in the countryside. At first it was very rare and a treat to get a bottle of lager with food, and even at the end of the eighties it was still possible to have no lager on the table and just make do with home-brewed beer. But in the nineties there was no one who would bring themselves to serve that."

The age of home brewing, which had lasted several hundred years, was over. A new era of industrial, brewery-produced beer had begun.

J.C. Jacobsen, the king of industrial brewers, who was of such importance for brewing in Europe during this period, would no doubt have been amused to know that in the twenty-first century home brewing would again become popular. Using specialised ingredients and equipment, people are now able to carry out their own experiments and tastings. Homes have once again become "brewhouses". Customs and practices may change over time, but one thing is sure: beer is here to stay.

BEER FOR SALE Although the Brewer was of the view that the beer sold itself if the quality was good, times have changed. Some of the advertisements which Carlsberg has used over the years have been produced by famous Danish artists and gained iconic status as well as constituting a piece of cultural history.

From the top left: *Carlsberg Breweries, J.C. Jacobsen – Copenhagen*, advertising sign, 1876 (Carlsberg Archive); *The Confirmand*, advertisement by Erik Henningsen, 1901-02 (Carlsberg Archive); *– and then a … Carlsberg*, Export poster by Thorkil Møller, 1957 (Carlsberg Archive); *"Sometimes you really need a Carlsberg"*, advertising campaign, 1987-89, created by Joe Petagno for the advertising agency Saatchi & Saatchi (Carlsberg Archive); *Our beer*, poster, 1999 (Carlsberg Archive); *Probably the best beer in the world*, international advertising campaign, 1986-2003 (Carlsberg Archive. Photograph: Bent Rej); *That calls for a Carlsberg*, international advertising campaign (Carlsberg Breweries 2011)

SOURCES

Andersen, H.C.: *H.C. Andersens dagbøger 1825-1875*, G.E.C. Gads Forlag, 1875

Bagge, Sverre: *Mennesket i middelalderens Norge*, Aschehoug, Oslo, 1998

Bech, Sv. Cedergreen et al.: *Københavns Historie*, vol. 4, 1830-1900, Gyldendal, 1982

Bligaard, Mette: *J.C. Jacobsen og Frederiksborg*, The Museum of National History, 1997

Christensen, Dan Ch.: *Naturens tankelæser – en biografi om Hans Christian Ørsted*, Museum Tusculanums Forlag, 2009

Fraenkel, A.: *Gamle Carlsberg 1847-1897*, H. Hagerups Boghandel, 1897

Francke, Børge and Andrup, Ernst: *Familien Jacobsen og Carlsberg*, Carlsberg Bladet 1959-63, Carlsberg Archive

Friborg, Flemming; Nielsen, Anne Marie; and Roepstorff, Sylvester: *Carl Jacobsens helligdomme*, Ny Carlsberg Glyptotek, 1998

Glamann, Kirsten (ed.): *Din hengivne Jacobsen, Bryggerens breve til sin søn 1850-70*, Gyldendal, 1995

Glamann, Kristof: *Bryggeren, J.C. Jacobsen på Carlsberg*, Gyldendal, 1990

Glamann, Kristof: *Carlsbergfondet*, Rhodos, 1976

Glamann, Kristof: *Øl og marmor, Carl Jacobsen på Ny Carlsberg*, Gyldendal, 1995

Glamann, Kristof and Kirsten: *Nordens Pasteur, fortællingen om Emil Chr. Hansen*, Gyldendal, 2004

Gyldendal & Politikens Danmarkshistorie, vol. 10

Harder, Thomas and Scheving, Hans: *Glimt af Rom*, Gyldendal, 2009

Hegner, Bonnie and Rindom, Jan: *Industrikultur i Danmark 1850-1914*, Skoletjenesten, 2007

Hude, Elisabeth: *Johanne Louise Heiberg og J.C. Jacobsen, Studier fra Sprog- og Oldtidsforskning*, G.E.C. Gads Forlag, 1964

Hyldtoft, Ole (ed.): *Kost og spisevaner i 1800-tallet*, Museum Tusculanums Forlag, 2009

Hyldtoft, Ole: *Dansk industri efter 1870*, 4, Odense Universitetsforlag, 1996

Jensen, Henrik: *Det faderløse samfund*, People's Press, 2006

Jørgensen, Jens Anker and Thomsen, Bente: *Gyldendals bog om danske klostre*, Gyldendal, 2004

Københavns historie, vols 3 and 4, Gyldendal, 1981

Lauring, Palle: *Bryggerne Jacobsen*, Høst & Søn, 1996

Lauring, Palle: *J.C. Jacobsen, Hans liv og gerning*, G.E.C. Gads Forlag, 1961

Letters and diaries of J.C. Jacobsen and Carl Jacobsen, Carlsberg Archive

Lindhardt, Jan and Uhrskov, Anders: *Fra Adam til robot, Arbejdet – historisk og aktuelt*, Gyldendal, 1997

Møller, Jan: *Borger i guldalderens København*, Sesam, 1999

Nielsen, Flemming Steen: *Højt skum, bryggerireklamer i kunst- og kulturhistorien*, Brandt's Museum of Media, 2008

Nielsen, Rolf: *Fra bonde til brygger, om Chresten, Jacob, Carl og tiden*, Forum, 1996

Nielsen, Rolf: *Politikens bog om øl*, Politikens Forlag

Nyrop, C.: *J.C. Jacobsen 1811-1911, et mindeskrift*, Carlsberg Foundation, 1911

Nørregaard-Nielsen, Hans Edvard: *Kongens København, en guldaldermosaik*, Gyldendal, 1985

Possing, Birgitte: *Viljens styrke, Natalie Zahle, en biografi om dannelse, køn og magtfuldkommenhed*, Gyldendal, 1992

Skougaard, Mette and Lyngby, Thomas: *Frederiksborg – Slot og Museum, Det Nationalhistoriske Museum*, Frederiksborg Castle, 2009

Tacitus, Publius Cornelius: *Germaniens historie, geografi og befolkning*, vol. 1 by Niels W. Bruun and Allan A. Lund, Wormianum, 1974

Thestrup, Poul: *Mark og skilling, kroner og øre*, Danish State Archives, 1999

Worsøe, Hans H. and Colding, Torben Holck: *Familien Jacobsen*, 1985

Aakjær, Jeppe: *Fra min bitte-tid*, 1928

Academy for Ancient Texts, www.ancienttexts.org
Danish Military History, www.milhist.dk
The Danish Academy in Rome, www.acdan.it
The Danish Beer Academy, www.olakademi.dk
Danish Beer Enthusiasts, www.ale.dk
The Danish Border Association, www.graenseforeningen.dk
Heimskringla, The Chronicle of the Kings of Norway, www.heimskringla.no